To

_____

From

_____

Date

_____

Incredible ANSWERS *to* PRAYER

More than a Coincidence…
True Stories of God's Miracles in Everyday Life

Guideposts
New York, New York

MYSTERIOUS WAYS: INCREDIBLE ANSWERS TO PRAYER

ISBN-10: 0-8249-3181-5
ISBN-13: 978-0-8249-3181-0

Published by Guideposts
16 East 34th Street
New York, New York 10016
Guideposts.org

Distributed by Ideals Publications, a division of Guideposts
2636 Elm Hill Pike, Suite 120
Nashville, Tennessee 37214

Acknowledgments

Every attempt has been made to credit the sources of copyrighted material used in this book. If any such acknowledgment has been inadvertently omitted or miscredited, receipt of such information would be appreciated.

"Healing Circle" is reprinted with permission from the author. Copyright © 2006 by Virginia Baker. All rights reserved.

"Wednesday Night Special" is reprinted with permission from the author. Copyright © 2005 by Jackie Scott. All rights reserved.

Scripture quotations marked (ESV) are taken from the Holy Bible, English Standard Version, copyright © 2001 by Crossway Bibles, a division of Good News Publishers. Used by permission. All rights reserved.

Scripture quotations marked (NAS) are taken from the *New American Standard Bible,* copyright © 1960, 1962, 1963, 1968, 1971, 1972, 1973, 1975, 1977, 1995 by the Lockman Foundation. Used by permission.

Scripture quotations marked (NIV) are taken from the Holy Bible, New International Version, NIV. Copyright © 1973, 1978, 1984, 2011 by Biblica, Inc. Used by permission of Zondervan. All rights reserved worldwide. www.zondervan.com

Scripture quotations marked (NKJV) are taken from *The Holy Bible, New King James Version.* Copyright © 1997, 1990, 1985, 1983 by Thomas Nelson, Inc.

Library of Congress Cataloging-in-Publication Data

Mysterious ways : incredible answers to prayer : more than a coincidence? : true stories of God's miracles in everyday life.
    p. cm.
  ISBN 978-0-8249-3181-0 (pearlescent casebound) 1. Prayer—Christianity—Anecdotes.
2. Miracles—Anecdotes.
  BV220.M98 2012
  248.3′2—dc23

                                        2012018417

Cover and interior design by Jeff Jansen/Aesthetic Soup | www.aestheticsoup.net
Cover photo by © Jojjik | Dreamstime.com.
Typeset by Aptara

Printed and bound in China
10 9 8 7 6 5 4 3 2 1

CONTENTS

CONTENTS

Contents

INTRODUCTION

Mysterious Ways: Incredible Answers to Prayer is the second book in our new series based on the *Guideposts* magazine column "Mysterious Ways." Once again we have collected some of the most uplifting accounts from our more-than-fifty years of publishing inspirational stories, to reveal how faith works supernaturally in ordinary lives.

In this collection you will see people just like you who are faced with impossible situations: hopeless health crises, rebellious children, bare cupboards, frightening automobile accidents.... Then see God intervene in amazing ways when hearts are lifted to Him in faith, trusting for His provision and help.

As you read these stories we hope you will remember that the same God who answered prayer in these accounts is able and willing to answer the prayers of your heart—no matter how impossible they may seem!

1
INCREDIBLE PROVISION

My God will meet all your needs according to the riches of his glory in Christ Jesus.

PHILIPPIANS 4:19 NIV

Heavenly Father, You are a faithful Provider. How amazing that no need we face is too trivial to bring before You, no problem too complicated. We praise You for Your great love!

MIRACLE STEW

by Adele Hooker

────── ∿ ──────

I've always had a strong faith in God, but I had never looked for miracles in my life. Until years ago...

When our family of four lived in Muskogee, Oklahoma, our income was so small we could barely pay for necessities. Sometimes it was cornflakes and milk for a week. On one such occasion, friends traveling through town stopped in, and to my amazement, my husband invited them for dinner.

I fidgeted, then went into my bedroom, knelt down and asked God how I was to cook a dinner with no food in the house.

"But you have," came the answer that formed in my head. "You have meat in the freezer." (I didn't believe it.) "You have vegetables." (Maybe a can of beans.) "Make a stew. And you have flour. Make biscuits." (That I could do. I'm a good biscuit builder.)

I went to the kitchen to prove my inner voice wrong, but there in the freezer lay a small amount of hamburger; in the crisper lay half an onion and a carrot; and in the bin under the sink were two small potatoes.

I made the stew. Hadn't I asked God for help? What could I do but follow the directions that seemed to come to me? I put the flimsy fare in a pot, mixed up the biscuits, then set the table.

When I took up the stew there was barely enough to fill a medium-size serving bowl; I thought my husband and I would eat only biscuits and milk. But when I passed the stew around, behold, there was plenty. I served us and passed the bowl around again!

When our dinner was over, the guests thanked me for the delicious meal. And I gathered up leftovers.

We had leftovers. We did, we really did!

BEST SEAT IN THE HOUSE

by Bonnie Kidder

I almost hadn't come to the class at church that night. With four kids and a full-time teaching job, I had plenty to do. But my eleven-year-old son Brady was having surgery the next day. I hated to think of him alone in the operating room. I'd been praying for weeks, asking God to be with Brady and his doctors during surgery, but it didn't feel like enough.

Standing in the doorway of the church hall, I couldn't believe how many people had shown up for this class. It looked like more than a hundred were seated at the tables scattered throughout the hall—but not a familiar face among them. No one I could ask to pray with me for Brady. I sat down at a table next to a dark-haired man, but the instructor immediately asked us to move. "Let's fill in all these vacant chairs up front," she said. The dark-haired man got up to look for another seat. I crossed the room to an empty chair. But just as I got there, someone else took it. I spotted another chair at the next table. The same thing happened again. And again. *I did not come here for a game of musical chairs*, I thought as I made a beeline for another chair. I flung myself into it and turned to see . . . the same dark-haired man I'd left behind.

"We meet again," he said as the instructor stood to speak.

"Tonight I thought we'd talk about our lives outside of church," she said. "Everybody share with the people at your table how you work your faith into your daily life."

The dark-haired man said, "I'm an anesthesiologist. Before I put a patient under, I pray for him. I ask each patient if they'd like to pray too. I used to be embarrassed about this . . . ."

"I think it's wonderful!" I interrupted. "My son is having surgery tomorrow. I'd feel so much better if his doctor could pray with him."

"Where is his surgery?" he asked.

I mentioned the hospital. "Dr. Duplechain is doing the operation."

"Then I can assure you that your son will be surrounded by prayer," he said, "because I'm the one scheduled to be taking him into the operating room."

In a room full of strangers, God had seated me—twice!—next to the one man who could pray with me that night and with my son in the morning.

Directory Assistance

by Beth Ann Batt

———— ◦◦◦◦ ————

We live on an island in Lake Erie, and during tourist season work is booming. But winter is a lean time for my husband and me. One November several years ago I worried about how we were going to make our car insurance payment.

I am not one to pray for things. So it surprised me when I got the idea that all I had to do was ask God for help. I sat down at the kitchen table and cleared my mind. Then I let my thoughts flow freely. *Lord, please send me work*, I prayed. *I will put my heart into anything that's given me. And if You can, make it something I can do with my children tagging along.* I focused all of my being on my request for a little while. Then, feeling peaceful, I let it go.

Not even half an hour later the phone rang. "Do you know anyone interested in delivering phone books on our island?" a woman asked.

"Me!" I almost yelled. She gave me more details. A few days later I met with the district manager, and he hired me on the spot. Curious, I asked how his company had come to call me for the job.

"Call you?" he said. "We only advertised this position in the mainland paper."

That afternoon I set out, four-year-old Jacob and nine-month-old John in tow. Together we delivered six hundred phone books door-to-door. Within two weeks my paycheck arrived—exactly enough to cover our car insurance. I wasn't surprised. I knew someone had my number.

FOR THIS CHILD I PRAYED

by Pamela Freeman

My husband and I sat at our dining-room table filling out the forms that would decide the future of our family. For two years, we'd tried to have a child. But infertility forced us to rethink our plans. We'd prayed and prayed about what to do and every sign had led us here, to this form that would officially start the process of adopting a child from Russia. Now I felt an incredible, powerful surge of confidence that we were doing the right thing. I signed the bottom and wrote the date, March 17, 2004.

That confidence carried me through the grueling months ahead. Costs for background checks, processing fees and other requirements were high. Putting together the documents that described us, our home, our health and our finances took months of paper chasing, visits from a social worker and repeated trips to government offices. Finally we completed everything and waited to hear from the adoption agency.

Then the Russian government changed its international adoption laws. What should have been a few months of waiting lasted more than a year. Had we really followed God's will? I started to wonder about the sense of confidence I'd felt the day we signed the forms.

In the spring of 2006, we got a call from the adoption agency. "There's a boy in one of our orphanages in southern Russia," the person said. "We're e-mailing you the pictures."

He was a sweet little redhead, two years old. It was love at first sight. We made our travel plans. Halfway across the world, in Volgograd, Russia, my husband and I found what we'd been praying for. The boy was shy at first, but soon he was playing and cuddling with us. I held him and didn't want to let him go.

"He has some minor medical problems," the orphanage director warned, reading through the boy's file. "We don't know who his parents were. He was abandoned when he was just a few weeks old."

I looked at my husband. Did any of that matter? He was meant for us, wasn't he? The director peered down at the boy's file again.

"He was found by a police officer," she said, "on March 17, 2004."

No Need Too Small

by Shirley Pope Waite

.... —w— ....

Two months after my husband graduated from school and started a new job, I gave birth to our first child. We had very little money and at times we had none at all.

The days went by and I eked out this and eked out that. Then one morning after I'd gathered up the baby's laundry, I found I'd run out of detergent. Our monthly paycheck wasn't due till the end of the week, and we barely had enough money left for our food needs, never mind soap. But I had to have clean diapers for my baby! It was one of those little frustrations that wells up to blimp-size discouragement.

"Oh, Lord, You know I need soap. I pray that my folks send me money—soon." My parents periodically sent a small check. They were the only source I could think of.

I heard a noise at the door. Could it be the mail carrier? Somehow I actually expected God would answer me that quickly. I glanced out the window, but no mailman. It must have been the wind rattling the screen.

I went on with my housework. I kept crying out to the Lord. "What will I do about these diapers? Oh, Lord, what will I do?"

Then suddenly I felt prompted to go to the front door. Perhaps the carrier had come and I'd missed seeing him. Perhaps a check . . .

I opened the door and hanging on the handle was a plastic sack containing a sample box of a new detergent!

What did I learn about prayer that day? That God not only answers prayers, but has His own way of chiding a too-frantic housewife. Isaiah 65:24 (NIV) says, "Before they call I will answer; while they are still speaking I will hear."

*H*EAT *R*ELIEF

by Theresa Corbley Siller

I hung up the phone, about ready to scream. I'd
made fourteen calls in the past half hour trying to
find someone to fix our broken air conditioner. That
repairman was the last one in our service area. Living
here in Florida, you get used to the heat. On an ordinary day I'd pour some iced tea and be patient. But
today was different.

My husband Rich had just been released from the
hospital after hip surgery. I went into his room where
he sat on the bed, propped up by pillows. "Are they
coming to fix it?" he asked, trying to sound cheerful.
But I could hear the pain in his voice.

"I'm still looking," I said. "In the meantime, let's
get a fan on you."

I reached up to the top shelf of the storage closet
and pulled down a heavy old oscillating fan. I bal-
anced it on a chair and angled it toward Rich. His

sweaty hair blew limply in the breeze. "That's great," he said, but he looked miserable. The fan only pushed the hot air around. His hip was hurting and the pain pills were making him nauseous. *Does he have to suffer through this heat too, Lord?* I fumed.

It was so unfair, I could barely stand to look at him. I marched out of the room and right out the front door. *I really am going to scream!* I thought, and I didn't want Rich to hear me. Out in the yard I raised my face to the burning blue sky. *I ought to pray*, I thought, but mad as I was, if I opened my mouth I didn't trust what might come out of it! So I counted to ten and went back into the house to make Rich a cold compress.

I'd barely gotten inside when the phone rang. It was our friend Raul. He didn't know about Rich's surgery and called just to see how we were doing. "Well, I'm mad as heck and Rich is miserable," I confessed, and told him about the surgery and the air conditioner.

"A buddy of mine just got a brand-new air conditioner," Raul said. "His old one still works fine. I can bring it right over to you."

By evening our house was nice and cool. Rich drifted off to sleep to the gentle hum of the air conditioner. I blushed to remember my earlier anger. God had answered the prayer I was too mad to make. Now that's cool!

In Tough Times

by Yvonne Willis

You know the saying: "Two steps forward and three steps back"? That pretty much summed up my life as a single mom. I was raising two teenagers on a teacher's aide's salary. It wasn't nearly enough to cover the bills, so I moonlighted as a waitress. Every time I thought that I had found a solution to my money worries, something would fall through and I would end up feeling worse off than before.

The latest setback? The new job I'd applied for—the job I'd prayed to get, the job I just had to get—went to someone else.

I don't know what to do, Lord, I prayed that night, sobbing in my family room. *Please tell me things are going to be okay.*

The next evening at the restaurant I tied on my apron, wishing I could be home with my kids. I walked up to my first table. A cheerful older couple. The woman gave me a smile that warmed me. I couldn't help but notice her unusual glass ring. "What a beautiful ring," I said.

We chatted for a minute then I took their order and left. When I came back with their drinks, the woman held out her ring. "God told me to give this to you," she said.

"Oh no, I couldn't," I said, embarrassed.

She gently placed the ring in my hand and closed my fingers around it. "It's yours," she said. "God also wants me to tell you things are going to be okay."

Right there at their table in the middle of the restaurant I broke down in tears. I told her that I'd asked God for those very words. "Thank you for giving me hope," I said.

Long after that night, that sense of reassurance stayed with me. I knew the right job would come in time.

Nine months later it did. I got a better position at another school and I started waitressing at a restaurant where I worked shifts that allowed me to spend more time with my kids.

Now in these tough times, I have money worries again, but they don't get me down. I know things will turn out okay. And when I wear that unusual glass ring, I'm reminded I'm not alone. I know God is always one step ahead, providing for my every need.

Not So Far Away

by Barbara Marrine

———— ⌘ ————

Hurry, Mommy, let's go trick-or-treating!" My daughter waited by the door in her pink princess costume while I paced the living room. Usually I liked taking her out on Halloween, but this year, I was a wreck. I was worried sick about my mother, who was in China on a vacation. Some vacation! I got a call that afternoon that she had slipped and fallen on the marble floor of her hotel and broken her hip. She was taken to a Beijing hospital. Mom was nervous because she couldn't understand any of the doctors. If only I could do something to help her!

"Mommy..." I knew I couldn't let my worries ruin my daughter's fun. *There's nothing I can do for Mom except pace and pray,* I thought. We left the house and headed down the block. I was so distracted, I barely took note of all the costumed kids around me. The sooner my daughter filled her bag with goodies, the sooner I could get back to my pacing.

A blinking red light approached through the darkness. It was a pumpkin-shaped pin attached to the coat of a man whose son I'd once given piano lessons to. "Hello there," I said, greeting him and the little cowboy at his side.

"Hello," the father answered. "Having fun?"

"I'm trying," I said.

"Why, what's wrong?" he asked.

I told him the whole story. My mother, in China, breaking her hip. Not understanding any of the doctors. "And I'm too far away to do anything!" I said.

He raised his eyebrows. "Beijing, you said?" he asked. I nodded.

He pursed his lips then smiled. "Believe it or not, my sister is a doctor at an English-speaking hospital there. If you want, I'll make a call right away and we'll try and get your mom transferred."

A few days later I sat on the living room floor with my daughter as she finished the last of the candy. "Mommy, how far away is China?" she asked.

"Not as far as I thought," I said.

JOY IN THE JOURNEY

by Donna Meyer

————————————————

I never thought I'd end up a dishwasher at a fast-food restaurant. I had a master's in early childhood education! But I hadn't gotten a full-time job, and substitute teaching just wasn't covering the rent.

So there I was on a warm evening one summer, up to my elbows in hot water. My feet ached and I kept thinking about all the debt I had. Suddenly, a phrase my mom liked to say popped into my thoughts: "When there's nothing else to do, pray." Wouldn't hurt to try. *God, please give me a new job, teaching kids. That's what I thought You wanted.* Over the next few days, I made a game of it. Each time I washed a pan lid, I said my prayer. I wound up praying for myself a lot.

One day, as I collected trays to take back to the kitchen, a woman came in, looking downtrodden. I asked her if she was okay. "I'm heading to Florida to take care of my mom," she said. "It's a lot of responsibility."

"I'm sure you'll do a great job," I said. I carried the trays to the kitchen, thinking of the woman and the many others who came through each day. Standing there next to the sink, I felt that all those prayers for myself were a bit selfish. *I know what I'll do. Each time I wash a tray I'll say a prayer for the person who used it.*

Over the coming weeks I actually stopped dreading my job and started enjoying my coworkers. Soon, working at the restaurant didn't seem so bad.

Eventually I got the job of my prayers—teaching elementary kids. But I was sad to leave the restaurant. Mom was right. When there's nothing else to do, pray. She could've added, "It changes everything." Even a job washing dishes.

HOME FREE

by Laura J. Shank

⸻ ⚬⚬⚬ ⸻

One spring I was desperate to move. I was a single mom, raising twin boys Ben and Robert, eleven, and daughter Catherine, nine. We had an old, water-damaged mobile home, and our neighborhood, surrounded by boarded-up office buildings and busy roads, wasn't safe. Nearby, in Flushing, it was a different story. There was a beautiful park where I often took the kids. Though I prayed about moving, I didn't have time to look. Then one day Ben came home with red welts on his neck. "What happened?!" I asked.

"I got beat up on the playground," Ben said. "But don't worry. I'm used to it." *Used to it?* I thought. That night I sat at the table and pored over the classifieds. *We have to get out of here. Fast.*

A few weeks later I met with real estate agents in Flushing. Soon I'd found the perfect home in a beautiful community. It had three bedrooms, a big kitchen and two bathrooms. The seller was anxious to make a deal, but there was one problem: The price was two thousand dollars more than I had. I had to walk away.

The next Sunday I sat in church, wondering what to do. Then the pastor spoke about prayer and how it leads us to accept what God has for us. *Lord*, I prayed right then, *if this water-logged home is where You want my kids and me to live, then so be it. But help me understand why. If it isn't, please guide me to the right place.*

The next day I took the kids to Flushing for lunch. I sat there, sick we couldn't move. Then I saw a copy of the local paper. I grabbed it and flipped to the classifieds. Listed was the same home I'd hoped for. Except the price had dropped by two thousand dollars!

A few weeks later, not only had I purchased that home, but I'd also found a buyer for my old place. When it's right to make a move, God will clear the way. All I had to do was ask.

In Good Hands

by Wanda Rosseland

I sat in silence beside Mom's hospital bed, not even the oxygen tank whirring now. It, along with her medications, had been removed from the hospice room. Soon it would be over. Tears filled my eyes as I gently stroked her hand. I felt so alone.

In six short weeks Mom had gone from a cheerful octogenarian piecing together a bright red-and-blue quilt to a still, silent form lying beneath it. I felt so helpless. Whenever I'd needed something, Mom had been there. Now, when she was barely clinging to life, there was nothing I could do. Mom was in the hands of doctors and nurses I didn't know. I yearned for someone to care for her the way she'd always cared for others, with kindness and love.

Please, God, I prayed, *please send Mom the right person to look after her.*

I hadn't eaten all day. I got up from my place by her bedside, walked down the hall to the cafeteria and picked up some soup. Across the room I saw a nurse getting her fork and napkin from the counter. Something in her face caught my attention. Who is that? Then it hit me. Angie Pawlowski. My treasured babysitter way back from when our kids were little. They loved to have her come over and play, and my husband and I never worried, knowing they were in such great hands.

"Angie," I said, giving her a big hug, "how are you? It's been years!"

"Why are you here?" she asked.

"My mom's in the hospice room," I said, feeling my eyes welling with tears.

"It's your mom in the hospice room?" she said softly. "Oh, Wanda, I'm the one caring for her."

That's when I knew. God had answered me before I'd even asked, providing the perfect care for my mother's last days. Yes, we were both in God's hands.

2
*I*NCREDIBLE *H*EALING

*B*less the Lord, O my soul; and all that is within me,
bless His holy name! Bless the Lord, O my soul, and
forget not all His benefits: Who forgives all your in-
iquities, Who heals all your diseases, Who redeems
your life from destruction, Who crowns you with lov-
ingkindness and tender mercies.

PSALM 103:1–4 NKJV

*Precious Savior, You are our Healer. Thank You that when
we face health crises of any kind we can run to you,
the Great Physician, and trust Your loving care in our lives.*

In Sight

by Jamie Cantrell

———— ∙∙∙ ————

"What will happen to me?" my husband said, sitting on the couch, a bandage covering his eyes.

I shook my head and said, "We'll just have to see what the doctor says tomorrow."

Earlier that week a chemical had shot into Ron's eyes at the plant where he worked. We were told the covering on his eyes should grow back in twenty-four hours. But Ron's eyes only grew worse. Now the doctor warned us Ron could go blind.

How can I raise two young kids and care for a blind husband? I worried, feeling hopeless. All Ron had ever needed were reading glasses. Now he might . . .

The next day we returned to the eye clinic. The waiting room was packed. A nurse took us to a room and asked Ron to read letters on an eye chart. "I can't get past the second line," Ron said.

"What needs to grow in Ron's eyes to cure him?" I asked the nurse.

"Epithelium," she said, then left the room. *God*, I prayed, *I've never needed You more*. I turned to Ron, mustered up all my courage and said loudly, "Epithelium, grow!" My face turned red as patients in the waiting room stared in through the open door.

Minutes later the doctor came in. "How do you feel?" he asked.

"Better," Ron said, smiling. The doctor looked at him quizzically and then positioned a scary piece of equipment and used it to peer into Ron's eyes. Finally he sat back. "Well, I'll be," he said. "I see epithelium growing."

Within a week, my husband's vision was back to normal. In fact, his eyesight improved so much he got rid of his reading glasses. As for me, I got rid of something even better—any doubt I may have ever had in the power of prayer.

THE GIRL WHO WAS FROZEN SOLID

by Jean Hilliard Vig

————— ⁓ —————

I grabbed my purse and the car keys, threw on my new green waist-length parka, and started toward the door. Mom called, "Jean, aren't you going to take your boots and snowmobile pants? It's supposed to get colder tonight."

I'd lived on a farm in northern Minnesota all my life and was used to cold weather. "I'll be fine, Mom. Just driving into town to meet some friends. It's not that cold."

I was nineteen years old and thought cowboy boots and blue jeans were more appropriate than warm clothing for a night out with friends. Besides, I had no idea that in just a few hours the temperature would plummet to twenty-five degrees below zero with gusts of fifty-mile-an-hour blizzard winds.

Around midnight, after a fun evening in Fosston with my friends, I was driving home in Dad's big white Ford LTD. I usually took the four-wheel-drive pickup, but tonight it was low on gas and Dad had said I could take the car.

Heading home, the snow sparkled festively in the beams of my headlights. I decided to take the old country gravel road because it was a few miles shorter than the blacktop. Besides, I had always loved that road. It meandered through a forest of tall pines. Every couple of miles a house or a farm dotted the landscape, but the rest was pure picture-postcard scenery—icy-blue Minnesota lakes, tall trees and the narrow, winding, hilly gravel road.

I didn't see the small patch of ice in the middle of the road because of the new snow. Before I knew what was happening, the car skidded off to the side and the front wheel slid precariously close to the ditch. I tried to back up slowly, but the tires were spinning. When I put the car in forward gear the front tire slipped off the shoulder and the car became helplessly marooned. I wasn't frightened, but I sure was disgusted! I could just hear Dad's booming voice when he found out what I'd done with his good car.

I knew there was a house a half mile or so ahead, so I got out of the car, slammed the door and stomped off down the road, forgetting my hat on the front seat. I was steaming over the mess I had gotten myself into, and my anger kept me warm for a few hundred feet. The wind forced me to zip up my jacket collar over my nose and mouth. I shoved my hands deep into my pockets and dug into the snow in my pointy-toed leather cowboy boots.

I walked on a little farther and then remembered Wally's place, in the opposite direction. It should be just a half mile or so, I thought. Wally was an acquaintance of my folks and I knew he had a four-wheel-drive truck and could pull my car out of the ditch easily.

As I passed the car, I felt like kicking the tire, but I trudged on. After a half mile or so, I passed a house. It was dark and there were no tracks in the driveway. Probably out of town, I thought. I walked on another half mile or more. The next house was also dark and the driveway filled with snow without a tire track to be seen. (I found out later that both of these families were home that night and that the wind had blown the snow over all the tracks an hour or so before I became stranded.)

I pressed on. The wind whipped and whistled through the pines. My feet were starting to bother me. My dressy high-heeled cowboy boots were not meant for hiking. Why hadn't I listened to Mom and taken my warmer boots? Where was Wally's house, anyway? I thought it was just over the next hill. I kept walking, but the fronts of my legs, protected only by my thin blue jeans, were aching from the cold. Down another hill. Why had I taken the shortcut? At least on the blacktop there'd be cars on the road this time of night.

I struggled up another hill. Finally, I thought I saw Wally's farm in the distance. Yes! There was the long lane leading to his house. I was breathing harder. And then . . . I blanked out. Although I don't remember it, apparently I half walked, half stumbled, falling at times, down that long lane. I crawled the last hundred feet or so on my hands and knees, but I don't remember doing that either.

By now, the wind chill factor was seventy to eighty degrees below zero. Right at Wally's front door I collapsed and fell face forward into the snow. And that's where I lay all night.

The next morning Wally came out his front door just before seven o'clock. Normally he didn't go to work until eight, but thank God, he decided to go in early that morning. Wally saw my body in the snow, leaned down and tried to find a pulse. There was none.

My swollen face was a gray, ashen color. My eyes were frozen open. I wasn't breathing.

Wally still doesn't know how he managed to pick me up and get me into his car. He said it was like struggling with a 120-pound cordwood stick or a big piece of meat out of the freezer.

At the hospital in Fosston, Wally yelled through the emergency room doorway for help. He picked me up under my arms and a couple of nurses lifted my ankles. My body didn't bend anywhere. As they were putting me on a stretcher, one nurse exclaimed, "She's frozen solid!" Another nurse, the mother of one of my best friends, said, "I think it's Jean Hilliard! I recognize her blonde hair and the green jacket!"

Mrs. Rosie Erickson, who works in bookkeeping, ran out in the hall when she heard the commotion. She leaned over my body. "Wait! Listen!" A hush fell around my stretcher. "It's a moaning sound . . . coming from her throat! Listen!"

I was wheeled into the emergency room. Dr. George Sather, our family doctor, was on duty that morning. He was unable to hear any breathing or a heartbeat with his stethoscope. Then he attached a heart monitor, which picked up a very slow, faint heartbeat. A cardiologist said it seemed to be "a dying heart."

"We have to get these boots off! Bring some blankets! She's still alive!" The emergency room sprang to life. My boots and jacket were the only clothing items they could get off immediately. The rest of my clothes were frozen on me.

When they cut my jeans off, the staff saw that my feet were black and there were black areas on my legs and lower back. My feet and legs were swollen. The tissue damage seemed so severe that when my parents arrived Dr. Sather told them that if I did live, my legs might have to be amputated. He wanted my parents to be prepared.

Dr. Sather ordered oxygen, and a nurse suggested trying Aqua-K-pads. Just the day before, a new kind of water-filled heating pad had arrived at the hospital. Quickly the nurses unpacked one heating pad box after another. Fortunately the only nurse on the staff who knew how to connect them to the special water-filled machines was on duty and she directed the operation. My body was frozen so hard that they couldn't pierce my skin with a hypodermic needle. There was no way at first to give me any medication to speed the thawing process or to prevent infection.

Mom, who was completely bewildered at the scene before her, answered quickly, "Yes . . . please do!"

Mrs. Erickson hurried to her office and made a phone call to the prayer chain chairman at the Baptist church where her husband is pastor. The prayer chain was set in motion. The first person on the list called the second. That person called the third and so on.

My heart started beating slightly faster. Even though still far slower than the normal rate of about seventy-two times a minute, the doctors were overjoyed. Slowly I started breathing on my own.

The prayer chain was lengthening. Mrs. Erickson called the pastors of the Lutheran, Catholic, Methodist and Bethel Assembly churches in Fosston. They, in turn, called the chairmen of their prayer chain groups, who passed the word along.

During the first hours that the prayer chain was underway, my legs and feet, instead of getting darker as Dr. Sather expected, started to lighten and regain their natural color.

One after another, the doctors and nurses filed in to marvel at the pinkish tinge appearing at the line of demarcation where the darkness started. (That was the line on my upper thighs where Dr. Sather said he thought they might have to amputate.)

The prayer chain spread to the nearby towns of Crookston and Bemidji, and Grand Forks, North Dakota. Soon hundreds, then thousands of people were aware that a young woman had been brought in to the Fosston hospital frozen solid and was in desperate need of God's miraculous healing.

One of the nurses, on her way to get more blankets, poked her head into Mrs. Erickson's doorway and said, "She might make it! Her legs are starting to regain color at the top! And her heart is beating stronger!" Mrs. Erickson looked up at the clock and thought, *The prayer chain is in full swing now. God is answering those prayers already. Of course, she's going to make it!* At that moment the whole attitude in my hospital room changed. Now, instead of "She probably won't survive" the feeling was "Perhaps she'll live, but she will surely lose her legs from the knees down."

Before noon that day I stirred and moaned a word that sounded like "Mom." My mother and oldest sister Sandra stayed near my bed, holding, squeezing and patting my hands. "Jean, Jean, wake up! Jeannie, can you hear me? It's Mom. Sandra's here too. Jeannie, we love you. Jeannie, can you hear?" Around noon I mumbled a few words to them.

All over the area the prayer chain was continuing. By midafternoon I woke up and started thrashing in bed. The doctors told me later that I moaned and yelled so much that they were convinced I would have severe brain damage.

All day the nurses and doctors watched in amazement as the blackness in my legs and feet disappeared inch by inch.

By late afternoon Dr. Sather thought perhaps my legs would be saved and that only my feet might have to be amputated. A few hours later he was astounded to realize that perhaps it would be just my toes. In the end I did not lose any part of my body! Normal color and circulation came back to even the blackest parts of my legs, feet and toes.

Dr. Sather had also thought he would have to do numerous skin grafts where huge blisters covered my toes. But these places healed too, without skin grafting. Indeed, after watching my body become whole again, I am convinced that a miracle did occur. Even Dr. Sather said, "I just took care of her. God healed her."

The doctors kept me in the hospital seven weeks to make sure of my recovery from frostbite and to lessen the possibility of any infection in my toes. And that entire time I never once experienced any fear. I'm convinced it was the prayer chain that kept me calm and filled me with a positive faith that I would be healed.

Since the night I nearly froze to death I met a wonderful man, got married, and had two beautiful children. My husband, children and I live on a farm outside Fosston, and my life is a tranquil, happy one. But there isn't a day that goes by that I don't think about the night I nearly froze to death. I've become a different person because of that experience.

My family and I are much closer now. I appreciate every day I'm alive, I have an enormous respect for the power of prayer. I believe that the prayer chains saved my life. Thousands of people I didn't even know bombarded heaven with powerful prayer requests in my behalf, and against all medical odds I survived. I not only lived, I survived as a completely normal, whole human being without even so much as a skin graft. In fact, unlike most other people who have suffered from frostbite, I now experience no ill effects from the cold.

Urgent Prayer

by Wilma Cook

———— ⟋⟍⟍⟍— ————

*F*riday, 12:15 PM. There wasn't much time. That was clear. The doctor assured me the woman in the critical-care-unit bed was my daughter. But she looked nothing like Marianne, her skin covered in purple blotches, her face bloated. "Your daughter has probably been unconscious for twenty hours," the doctor said. "I don't have the expertise to diagnose her. I only know that if I can't find someone to treat her soon . . ." His voice trailed off.

Already a half hour had passed since I'd gotten the call. A maintenance man had found Marianne collapsed in her apartment, her two-year-old son, Jalen, nearby. Without putting down the receiver, I'd phoned my sister Mary Jane. I wanted her to go to Marianne's and get Jalen, and then pick up his brother, ten-year-old Levi, from school. Levi had been staying with us.

She needed to bring them to the hospital where my husband Stanley would watch them. And call my two sons. But first I needed her to... "Call the prayer team at church," I said. "Marianne needs their help!"

Now, as the doctor's words began to register, I wondered if Mary Jane had reached anyone. Would the prayers of a few people at a country church even matter? "Doctor," I said, "I'm not giving up. This momma needs her baby."

The doctor shook his head. "We're calling other hospitals. But we don't have much time."

I stood by Marianne, holding her limp hand, searching for an eye blink, a finger twitch, any sign of life. Something had gone wrong with her circulation. Beyond that the doctor was at a loss. "Can you hear me?" I whispered to my daughter. My heart cried out, *Please, God. Don't let my child die.* Over and over I prayed, but felt little comfort. The ventilator's rattle seemed to grow louder. Was anyone else praying? *God, keep her, make her whole.* Each time I said the words I could feel the minutes passing.

1:00 PM. Head bowed, I almost didn't notice when Kay, a friend from church, slipped into the room. "I got a message and came as soon as I could," she said. "There's ten of us down in the waiting room, praying and calling everyone we know. I need to get

back. I just want you to know we're here for you."
She gave me a small white cloth blessed by a minister
that another friend had brought by. I wove it through
Marianne's soft brown hair, then took her hand again
and continued my own silent prayers. *God, help her. Keep
her. Make her whole. God, help her...*, I pleaded, words tumbling over each other. I started massaging her arms
and legs, hoping I could restore some circulation.

2:00 PM. Where was the doctor? I wished I could
see Stanley, but he had to stay with Jalen and Levi. *And
I can't leave Marianne. She needs me here.*

Finally the doctor returned, grim-faced. "I've
reached four hospitals. But all of them say she's too
far gone to transfer. I'll keep calling. But at some
point we'll have to make a decision."

I stroked Marianne's puffy cheek. Could a mother's loving touch reawaken her? Was I praying for the
impossible? What if God was calling her home? What
if that was His will even if every cell in my body resisted it?

4:00 PM. Footsteps in the hallway. I looked up
to see the doctor. "We're airlifting your daughter
to a hospital in Huntington, West Virginia," he said
quickly. "I know it sounds like good news. But I have
to caution you. With the air-pressure changes and
stress of the transfer, she may not survive the flight."

Stanley, Levi and I nearly ran to the car, me holding little Jalen's hand. That drive up Interstate 64 took two hours, the longest two hours of my life. "I'm so afraid," Stanley said. "What if she doesn't make it?"

"We just have to have faith," I answered. I held my head in my hands, trying to block out my fears. I tried to picture Marianne, tried to imagine her healthy, going shopping with me again.

6:00 PM. Stanley dropped me off at the door of the hospital. A doctor met me at the ICU, his face serious. "Your daughter has a tumor inside her heart, throwing off blood clots," he said. "If we can get her to a specialized cardiac surgical hospital, there is a ten percent chance of survival. But it's only a matter of time before a clot hits a vital organ and kills her."

I'd been praying for more than six hours. Now, with the diagnosis, the odds seemed insurmountable. I took out my cell phone and called Kay. "Is the prayer chain still going?"

"Remember those missionaries from New Guinea who visited your friend's church?" Kay said. "Someone e-mailed them. They're praying for Marianne." New Guinea? I wasn't even sure where it was on a map, and now people there were praying for Marianne. No matter where they were praying, time was still slipping away.

Saturday 12:00 AM. Friday turned into Saturday. The doctor was still searching for a hospital that could do the difficult surgery. All those prayers, from people all over the world. Why is God waiting so long? Standing by Marianne, I massaged her legs again. They felt so cold. I pushed myself to keep praying, but it was a struggle just to keep my eyes open. I hadn't eaten since breakfast. I could feel myself growing weaker. It was one in the morning. The hospital was eerily still. Two o'clock. No word. Three. I jerked myself upright as I felt my eyes closing. Stay awake!

4:00 AM. The doctor burst into the room. "The Cleveland Clinic has agreed to take Marianne. We're flying her there within the hour." Stanley, Levi and Jalen were dozing in the waiting room. Cleveland was another six-hour drive. I called my oldest son, Kevin. He would come to Huntington and drive me to Cleveland. I hugged Stanley before he left to take Jalen and Levi back home to Arnett. "Keep praying," I said. Too nervous to sleep, I alternated between praying and sending thoughts to Marianne as Kevin drove. *Hang on. We're almost there.*

12:00 PM. We reached the Cleveland Clinic twenty-four hours after that first call. It's a massive medical complex, dwarfing anything back in Arnett. Kevin and I walked down corridor after corridor before we finally found Marianne and her doctor. "With surgery there's still a chance your daughter will live," he said. "But I can't make any promises about her quality of life."

"In Huntington they told us there was a ten percent chance," I said, my voice quavering. "Is there?"

His face grew serious. "Don't let anyone tell you the odds of life. She has a chance, but only God knows the odds."

I kissed Marianne on the cheek and removed the prayer cloth from her hair. It had been with her all the while. For the first time I felt a weight lift off me, like someone else was shouldering my burden. As the doctor followed Marianne's gurney out of the room I told him, "There are a lot of people praying for Marianne, so I just want you to know that you're in God's hands now."

The doctor turned back. "We're all in God's hands," he said.

In the waiting room I picked up my cell phone. There was a message from Kay: "Wilma, I've just been counting the e-mails I've received. Do you know there are people from more than 120 churches praying for Marianne? Vancouver, Washington; Troy, Michigan; Anchorage, Alaska; Tokyo; Jakarta. Our prayer chain has gone viral."

How many prayers had I said in the last twenty-four hours? I wondered. At least a couple thousand. What if I added in all the other people? A quarter million prayers? For one woman from a small country church, it was more support than I ever imagined possible.

4:00 PM. After four hours of surgery, the doctor found me in the waiting room, my head still bowed in prayer.

"We removed the entire tumor from Marianne's heart, so there's no danger of it shedding any more clots. She'll need more surgeries, so it's early yet. But things are headed in the right direction."

Then he smiled. "You tell your people to keep doing what they're doing," he said, "because I've done everything I can do today." My people. I thought about all those people praying for Marianne, in places I'd never heard of: Roan Mountain, Tennessee; Santee, California; Little Harbour, Newfoundland. I could see their faces, hundreds of people, maybe thousands. I felt like that guy on the cell-phone commercial. I had a prayer network behind me as far as the eye could see.

With God's blessing the doctors at the Cleveland Clinic performed a miracle. It would take another three months of therapy and recovery, but when

Marianne came home, she was able to walk in the door on her own, bend down and give Jalen and Levi a monster hug. I still think about all those prayers and the support each of us can give to one of God's children, whether in Arnett or across the world. We're connected, not just by technology, but by God's love, the most powerful network of all.

*H*EARTBEAT

by Billy Zilembo

············· —ᗰ— ·············

One July morning, I was on duty as a traffic enforcement officer with the Framingham, Massachusetts, Police Department. I had just begun my shift at eight o'clock when my police car radio crackled. "Billy," the dispatcher said, "swing over to the hospital to see your wife."

Tami and I were expecting our first child. She was three weeks past her delivery date, and every other day she'd been going to the hospital for a test to monitor the baby's condition. Our obstetrician, Dr. Gerald Cohen, had assured us the delay was not unusual.

The preceding year we had lost a baby through a miscarriage, so this time we'd been very careful. Tami had been going to our health club, had stopped dieting, had taken a less stressful job and had been taking vitamins. The two of us had enrolled in a natural-childbirth class so that I could be right there with her in the delivery room, coaching her. And we'd been praying for a healthy baby.

At Framingham Union Hospital Doctor Cohen was waiting. I was startled when he hugged me. *Uh-oh*, I thought, *he's going to tell me we have a beautiful new baby*.

Instead, he said in a strangled voice, "No, Billy, the baby hasn't come yet. And Billy, it doesn't look good. There's no heartbeat—nothing at all."

"You're kidding!"

"Billy, we tried two monitoring machines, but there's nothing. I listened with a stethoscope, so did another doctor. Nothing."

This was unreal. I couldn't accept it. "Is it possible there could be a machine malfunction?" I wondered out loud. "Could it be human error?"

He shook his head. "No, two machines can't be wrong. They have built-in monitors to detect mal-functions. These are multimillion-dollar systems."

So that was it. Our baby would be born dead. I couldn't let any emotion show, not a bit. Or I'd go to pieces.

When I went to Tami's room in the maternity ward, her friend Judy Blaine was with her. Tami reached up to embrace me. "I'm sorry, Billy. So sorry."

"It's all right, it's all right," I whispered as she clung to me. I kissed her tear-damp cheek.

"Will you be okay?" she asked.

"Sure. Will you?"

She tried to smile, but the corners of her mouth kept pulling down. "Just one thing. I want to see the baby when it comes. I want to hold it. Otherwise, Billy, we'll always be wondering what it looked like." Fighting for control, she said, "I want a lock of hair . . . and pictures too . . . ."

She lay there for a moment, then asked, "Billy, should we try to have another one right away?" Her eyes were brimming.

"Absolutely!" I said without hesitation.

Doctor Cohen had said they'd be taking Tami up to the operating room as soon as it was available.

Now we waited. The hospital's bereavement team came down to console us. The maternity ward was being renovated, and some of the construction workers in their sweat-stained T-shirts stopped to stare. Everybody, it seemed, knew about our baby.

I went out to find Doctor Cohen again. I wanted to tell him that Tami wanted to see our child.

When I came back, Tami was arguing excitedly with Judy, saying, "Something moved—I'm almost certain something moved."

"It was just gas," Judy said, shaking her head sadly. "Billy, she's getting herself all worked up."

"Honey," I said, sitting on the bed and holding her hands, "don't do this. Two machines didn't detect a heartbeat; two doctors couldn't, five nurses..."

"We can't give up now, Billy. We've prayed to God that our baby would be born healthy. We've got to expect a miracle. You've got to believe with me."

I could only shake my head.

"Come on!" she said, staring at her stomach, "I know you're alive in there. Now, don't you be a lazy baby. Move!" Then, coaxing, wheedling: "Please move, darling. Move for Mommy. Come on, let's show Daddy—"

"Tami, don't," I cried.

"You're alive. I know you are," Tami kept repeating. She would not give up. "Come on, don't be a lazy baby. We're going to have that miracle."

At about noon Tami was wheeled into the white-tiled operating room where the cesarean section would be performed. I was with her. They even let Judy in. "I'd like to see them try to stop me!" Judy muttered.

Dr. Cohen gave Tami a spinal. "God...last chance...," she murmured. The surgery began.

Dr. Cohen made a short horizontal incision on the lower abdomen, then clamped it. Seconds dragged by. I was gripping Tami's hand and Judy was gripping mine. The nurse, who was hugging me from behind, whispered, "Now you're going to see the baby. If you have to leave the room, I'll help you."

"No," I said, staring transfixed as a tiny head suddenly appeared between the doctor's hands. Amazing... In my police work, I had seen stillborn babies. They always looked grayish. This baby was pinkish-gray. Time stopped. The world stopped.

The assisting surgeon was saying, "Jerry...Jerry, I think we have life here."

There was a small sputtering, then a piercing cry.

"Dear God!" cried Doctor Cohen. "We do have life! Tami! Tami!"

"Is...that my baby?" Tami asked groggily.

"You better believe it is, sweetheart!" I cried, planting a kiss on her cheek.

The nurses began crying and hugging one another. One threw her chart in the air.

Then, after they cut the cord, the baby was being handed to me. A girl. I was stunned, holding this vigorous, squirming bit of life. Doctor Cohen leaned over and kissed Tami. "This is unbelievable!" he cried. "Unbelievable!"

Beside myself with joy, I clutched that struggling, wailing baby to me and started walking toward the double doors leading to the corridor. The nurses were on my heels.

"Mr. Zilembo! What are you doing?" They steered me back inside, where I surrendered our daughter. Doctor Cohen grabbed me and said, "I don't believe it! I can't explain it, but that baby is alive!"

"Do you—do you think she'll be normal?" I asked.

"Billy, on a scale of one to ten, most kids are six or seven at birth. I'm giving your baby an eight!"

I ran back out into the corridor, and as soon as the construction workers saw me, I began yelling, "She's alive! The baby's alive!"

Friends who were keeping vigil stared open-mouthed. My buddy, Jimmy, began crying like a baby. Construction workers pumped my hand and slapped my back. A priest got off the elevator, apologizing for being late. He had come to give the last rites. And right there, in front of everybody, I knelt in that hospital corridor and thanked God with all my heart.

Today, little Ami is a happy, healthy and dimpled darling. And where did her name come from? From the capital letters in the phrase that everyone used in talking about her—"A Miracle Infant." Our miracle baby. God's miracle.

A Different Answer

by Marion Bond West

———※———

I was driving home and thinking over and over, *There's nothing wrong with me*. This, despite the doctor saying there was, and then the bombshell he dropped: I would probably have to start giving myself shots.

Earlier I had sat across the desk from a pencil-thin rheumatologist wearing a blue button-down shirt. He had already advised me that the first appointment would take an hour and a half. I liked his messy desk; it resembled mine at home. I glanced down at the chart where he pointed. "Your X-rays and blood work indicate that you are in the early stages of rheumatoid arthritis," he said. "I'm going to prescribe some pills, but I expect you'll decide to give yourself regular injections."

"I don't think so," I said, smiling politely. My thinking was: So I've been diagnosed with RA. That doesn't mean that I actually have it. I took the prescription for pills and made another appointment for three months later. Well, whatever.

I pulled into our driveway at home and felt an increasingly familiar twinge in my hand when I turned off the ignition. Ow! Inside the house I dropped my keys and purse onto the kitchen counter. My husband Gene was full of questions. I put him off. "Here, let me see the pills you've got," he insisted. He sat down and began reading all the detailed paperwork the pharmacy had given me. I hate directions of any kind.

Early the next morning, during my quiet time, I wrote in my prayer journal, "Lord, I am sure this isn't a big deal. Just don't let the pain get worse—in fact, take it all away. I trust You to do that. I feel pretty good—most of the time."

The very next day Gene nagged, "Marion, I'm sure you should be exercising more now that you've been diagnosed. Not long ago you walked four miles, then two, now it's . . ."

"I'll start back in the spring. I like early mornings."

"Come on. I'll walk with you now. It's nice outside."

"Not now," I snapped, walking away.

Toward the end of the first year, the pain became worse, so intense it exhausted me. My hands and thumbs hurt most of the time. Turning the ignition in the car one day, I yelped in pain. I had to rest both hands in my lap. Finally, blinking back tears, I started the car.

My feet hurt, as did my back. Gene and I curtailed many activities. My energy level drained to zero. So did creativity, enthusiasm—and joy. Many mornings I crawled to the bathroom in the dark for my medications. I kept them under the sink so I didn't have to bend down or put weight on my hurting feet.

At a regular three-month checkup, my doctor asked right off, "How's your pain?" It sounded more like an ambush than a question.

"So, so," I mumbled.

Making sudden eye contact, he asked, "And are you still crawling to the bathroom?"

I could've kicked myself for having admitted that to him in a previous conversation. "Sometimes," I said.

"Are you walking and getting regular exercise?" he persisted.

"No."

"Did you read the brochure I gave you about the injections?"

"Not all of it." Actually, I hadn't even opened it. There was some energetic, outdoorsy looking gal on the cover. She trudged up Pike's Peak or some such mountain, making it look like super fun. The picture of health. Obviously, she gave herself the wondrous regular injections. "Don't these shots cost a lot of money?" I asked, hoping for an out. In fact, I couldn't imagine injecting myself even if someone paid me to do it.

"I've got hundreds of patients who use these shots to treat RA."

I mentioned the injections to Gene. He beamed. Looked relieved. "Then you must try them. You're spending almost all of your time on the sofa or in bed. I want my walking buddy back, honey."

Over and over I prayed and wrote in my prayer journal, "Lord, please take this pain away. I want my life back. I don't know what to do." I sat there in my prayer chair, hurting and no longer even trying to fight off depression.

I'm trying to tell you what to do, Marion.

Two hot tears plopped down onto my journal. *I don't know if that's You, Lord, but in case it is, I'll do what I think You're saying.*

That week I had another appointment with my rheumatologist. I sat in the small, light green, familiar examining room, staring out the window. I'd brought along a book to read because my doctor only kept arthritis magazines in the room. I refused to read them. Maybe I didn't even have . . . Maybe I did. Turning a page in my book, I felt a sharp sneaky pain rip through my thumb. Sometimes I experienced the same pain when I squeezed out toothpaste. Would the shots really be as scary as what was obviously happening to me? Was it the medicine I really feared?

My doctor came in, brisk and efficient. After a routine exam, a few questions, he wrote out a prescription and laid it down on the table. "You need to consider this seriously. And you must start back walking." Then he handed me another brochure with the excited mountain girl on the cover. "You are about to begin your second year of RA. This medicine can help you and stop further bone damage. But it's not about the shots. It's about you. You have to participate in your treatment. You can't retreat into denial." He turned and walked out.

The decision was still mine. So was the constant pain. I decided to swing by our pharmacy and see what the prescription would cost. To my amazement, with the help of insurance and Medicare, not too much.

I was weary of thinking about me. My pain. My disability. The condition I'd tried to deny was now defining me. The more I tried to hide from it the more it was taking. Yet I'd thought denial was the best medicine—that to admit I was sick was to give up. It wasn't good that I had this disease. But God would help me by sending helpers—Gene, my doctor, even that pesky picture of health on the brochure. I longed to forget about myself; laugh, wake up anticipating plans for the day. Start my car. Even vacuum. Oh, I didn't want to let go of my stubbornness! I wanted God to heal me—without injections.

On a Wednesday at high noon, I sat alone in the kitchen reading slowly for the fifth time the instructions (remember I hate instructions) and studying the simple diagrams. The actual injection was more like flipping a light switch than giving myself a shot. No needle was ever visible. The discomfort resembled a brief muscle cramp. The brochure said that results could come as soon as the second week or take as long as three months.

But my relief was immediate. At last I'd surrendered. Not to a disease, though. I surrendered the stubbornness of my denial that was undermining my health more than the RA itself. Until I could admit I had the disease, I could never get better.

I'm back to walking with Gene. I have a newfound gratitude for pain-free days and for my determined rheumatologist. I'm reminded of people in pain 24–7 and I pray for them.

Today I wrote in my prayer journal, "Father, thank You for speaking through my husband, my doctor and others. I know I'm not always the easiest person to deal with. But isn't that the way You made me? All I've ever known is to be myself, Lord. I ask You now to help me be myself with RA."

Lord, Where Is My Miracle?

by Anne Fitzpatrick

$\mathcal{D}$ad's trouble started, innocently enough, with a sore toe. Just a nuisance, at first, but the stubborn infection resisted all healing efforts—hot soaks, dry heat, cutting out the front of his shoe to avoid pressure—nothing helped. The swollen, giant toe became a throbbing, painful fire that refused to go out. Pain etched new creases in Dad's lined face; his thin, silver strands of hair were often damp with perspiration.

In the hospital, after tests, the doctor told us, "Joe has severe arterial occlusion. The blood supply can't get there—that's why the toe doesn't heal."

Along with severe arthritis, poor circulation had been a fact of Dad's life for a long time, but was it as bad as all that? We looked to the wisdom of this young, highly recommended surgeon. "What can be done?"

He didn't waste words. "We have to get rid of the toe. Then hope the wound will heal."

Hope? We could do better than that. We could pray. Surely God could heal my father, and he could live without one big toe. *Just a small miracle please, God.*

It didn't work. The pain of an infected toe was nothing compared with that of its unhealed amputation. There were more consultations, more tests. An unthinkable possibility was in the back of all our minds, but no one said it out loud,

The doctor phoned one night, after hours; his crisp voice coming over the line seared painfully into my ear. "There's only one way to keep the infection from spreading. Do a further amputation, far enough up where we're pretty sure there'll be blood flow—just below the knee."

So cut and dried, so businesslike, as if he were discussing tree surgery. A diseased limb: was one so different from the other? My stomach—tied into knots against the thought—knew there was.

I fought to remain as controlled as the doctor. "We'll have to talk to him about it."

"Of course. But we can't wait too long."

I thanked him and hung up. Thanked him! I wept.

I went to my mother and told her what the doctor had said. Her expression didn't change; I thought she hadn't heard. But then a deep sigh told me she had absorbed it all, was holding painful thoughts inside herself, They are not demonstrative folk, my parents, but they are strong. How else could they have bravely made a new life all those many years ago in a strange land across an ocean, where people with ways so different appeared to speak gibberish?

Now Mom only said quietly, "I was afraid of that." And I could see her lips moving in silent prayer.

Dad himself accepted the news stoically, nodding. He'd known all along. "No use waiting, then. Might's well get it over with." His calloused hands were clenched on the bed rails.

But we, the children, weren't so ready. Huddled over a small table in the hospital coffee shop, my brother said, "I've arranged for another opinion." We'd heard of arterial bypass and other treatments. Pipe dreams, they turned out to be, and, one by one, like tenpins falling in a perfect strike, all hopes collapsed. But there was still God. He could deal with clogged arteries, even if no one else could.

The time was set. Outside Dad's room the doctor marveled at the way he'd taken the news. "But," he said soberly, "you have to realize . . ."

We waited. I almost felt sorry for this doctor, seeing now that underneath his sometimes brusque manner, none of this was easy for him either.

"Your father may not come through surgery. There's always a risk. And at his age, in his condition, well, he'll probably never walk again."

Because of his arthritis, Dad had begun using a cane several years before, then two canes; following a mild stroke only a year before, the man who'd always been so strong and vital reluctantly accepted the sturdier support of a walker. But not to walk at all! The thought alone might kill him.

My younger sister, as fiery as her father in the face of the impossible, said sharply, "Don't ever tell him that! He's going to want to try, and he'll do it."

The doctor didn't argue, but there was sadness in his eyes.

Early in the morning Dad was wheeled into surgery. Mom held his hand until the last possible moment, then we all kissed him, and I said good-bye to my miracle-wish. In the waiting room my prayers were rambling, confused. Was anyone listening?

It was done. Hours later, back in his room, Dad was surprisingly alert, his eyes darting about as he watched nurses checking his heart, blood pressure, IV. Suddenly his heartbeat accelerated . . . visibly, alarmingly. The activity around him increased; there was much scurrying about, barking of orders down a chain of command. They raced him, bed and all, to the cardiac unit, where he was put on a monitor. A heart specialist was summoned. All the resources of the hospital were being called on, while I silently cried, *God, where are You?! What kind of miracle is this?*

At last Dad's condition stabilized and the crisis passed—but into more days of endless pain. My father had survived World War I and its wounds, and years of pick-and-shovel construction work, never tiring, never complaining, but he'd never had to endure anything like this. Sometimes he cried, apologizing for squeezed-out tears; he wasn't used to them and they embarrassed him.

He prayed. I never knew, really, about his relationship with his God. Dad had always been a private man, in the old-country manner, never talking about difficult things. But his well-worn prayer book was always with him, and when people from church came to pray he seemed calmer . . . peaceful, somehow, inside himself, and his hands on the bed covers were still.

Days passed before the doctor felt sure enough to say, "The stump is healing. It looks good." Dad nodded, the trace of a smile lighting his tight features. "Thank you, doctor," he said, his old voice strong with respect for this capable young man.

Our relief was like wind sighing through willows; I felt as if I'd been holding my breath for a very long time. *Thank You, God.*

But Dad's ordeal was far from over. There were still long weeks of therapy ahead, more pain, the enormous task of learning to walk on an artificial leg with a body that still ached with arthritis—which, of course, remained unchanged.

"It'll be brand-new, Dad," we joked. "Better than your old leg," But secretly we wondered, *Will he be able to walk again?*

He grew stronger, and therapy began. Dad waited eagerly for the sessions; there was much to be done before he'd be ready for the new leg. In the therapy room he walked along parallel bars, hopping on his right leg, building strength. Back in bed, he did extra sets of the exercises he'd been taught, his expression intent, determined.

On the weekend, when no therapy was scheduled, he persuaded nurses to help him walk from his room, setting a goal a short distance down the hall. He could use his walker, in a hop-step style. I thought of the doctor's dark prediction, He'll probably never walk again, as Dad cheerily called back to his roommate, "Good-bye, John, I'm leaving!"

We laughed, the sound overly loud in the small room. It was a beginning.

The new leg was ready. But it didn't look all that great, it was so heavy, and it was hard to make it work. The therapist, a lovely young woman, younger than some of his grandchildren, encouraged Dad patiently, lovingly and, as she saw his determination, admiringly. "That's fine, Joe," she'd say. "Keep up the good work! I'm proud of you."

Dad smiled at her, appreciating her hard work. "I will," he said. "I will." He knew he had to master this alien limb, make it a working part of his body, before he could go home—his one overriding goal.

He was discouraged at times, even depressed. The sparkle in his eyes was dulled by pain and concentration; there was no room in his mind for the usual lively interest he had in TV shows and daily news. But though he may have been down, he was never out. Less than three weeks from the day he first put on his new leg, we brought him home.

As I watched him walk about the rooms, almost as well as before, only a little slower, leaning more for support on the walker, I thought about the miracle I had prayed to God for, the one He had chosen not to grant.

But was this so?

The more I thought about it the more I knew that God had answered, not with one miracle, but many. There were those of medical science and technology— though faced with gigantic problems, God's workers still found ways around them. Doctors, nurses, therapists, aides—where did their skill and dedication come from if not from God? Dad's own courage to face each difficult day—wasn't that a gift from God? Most of all there was my mother who, in spite of her own fragile health, was always there, holding Dad's hand, bringing her homemade soup, constantly praying. Who but God could have given her such loving compassion?

Yes, He'd heard our prayers and answered them abundantly. *Thank You, God, for all of them, and help me to continue seeing Your loving Hand at work in all life's daily miracles, large and small.*

Pray for Baby Layne!

by John Howard

—⦿—

Five thirty in the morning. Still dark out. I took a deep breath, the crisp November air chilling my lungs, and climbed into my Ford pickup. I didn't usually drive to work so early, but I had signed on for the morning shift at Lowe's, where I'm a manager. A couple of miles in I took a shortcut I hadn't used in a while, through a growing subdivision. I was surprised to see how many people had already put their Christmas lights up.

There was a brilliant glow up ahead, almost beckoning me through the darkness. Must be one of those new high-tech decorations, I thought. Then I got closer. This was no decoration. It was a sign. A roughly cut piece of plywood, maybe four by three feet, painted white, with a message bathed in floodlights: PLEASE PRAY FOR BABY LAYNE.

Questions bounced around in my mind: Who was this child? What was wrong? Why would someone go to such great lengths to put up a lighted sign for prayer?

Maybe it troubled me because I had been wrestling with prayer for years. I envied people like my wife Susan. She prayed with such conviction. "Praying brings me closer to God," she'd tell me when I'd ask her about it. "You should try talking to Him more—He's a great listener."

But whenever I tried to pray, my words felt mechanical, so rote. God seemed so remote, so far away. How could I be sure He would answer? Or that He would even hear me?

I was about to drive away, but those words—"Please Pray for Baby Layne"—were staring at me. Challenging me, almost. All at once something came over me. "Lord, I know I haven't exactly trusted that You hear my prayers," I said. "But this isn't about me. Please heal baby Layne."

The next morning I got into my truck, grabbed a coffee at the drive-through and cut through the subdivision. There it was: that same sign shining through the dark. I put aside my doubts and said another prayer. *Lord, please bless the baby's family today.*

The day after that? You got it. I said another. Before long I had a new morning ritual: Drive. Get coffee. Pray for baby Layne.

A few weeks into it, I told Susan about the sign—and my praying.

"Isn't it nice to start your day off by thinking about someone else?" she said.

"I'm just doing what the sign says," I replied. "I wonder how baby Layne's doing now."

"Why don't you knock on their door and ask?" Susan said.

I didn't want to bother a family that was probably overwhelmed with caring for their sick child. So, instead, I just kept praying.

And something strange happened. One night, lying in bed, I closed my eyes. *Lord, You've given me so much. Thank You.* Then I caught myself. Did I just spontaneously pray? And it felt as natural as breathing! A sense of trust washed over me.

For the first time I felt like God was near, that He was listening to me. As if praying for baby Layne had opened up the lines of communication.

One spring afternoon I finally mustered up the courage to stop by the house in the subdivision. There was a man—about my age, fiftyish—in a white baseball cap, mowing the lawn. *Now's my chance*, I thought. I pulled into the driveway.

I got out of my truck. The man saw me and reached down to shut off the lawn mower.

"I'm John," I said, trying to find the right words. "I just wanted to tell you, I . . . I saw your sign a few months back and I've been praying for baby Layne ever since."

He didn't say a word, just stood there. *Uh-oh, I guess I shouldn't have come*, I thought.

Then the man's eyes pooled with tears. "I'm Kenny," he said. "Baby Layne is my grandson, and hearing that really means a lot, sir. Thank you." Then he reached out and gave me a bear hug. It felt a little awkward, but I didn't mind.

Kenny and I stood on the lawn and talked for a while. Baby Layne, he told me, had been born nearly four months premature—weighing just over a pound—and had undergone open-heart surgery.

"The doctors didn't think he would make it," Kenny said. "But I wanted to do something to help so I made the sign."

"I'm glad you did," I said. "Because there's another reason I came by today to talk to you."

"And what's that?" he asked.

"Well, praying for your grandson has really changed my life," I said. "I'm a lot closer to God now. I wasn't so close before."

"He does work in unusual ways, you know," Kenny said. "Just think, it took a real sign from God to get your attention!" He opened the front door. "C'mon in and meet Layne. He's doing great now."

Layne was on the couch with his grandmother, cradled in her arms. She handed him to me. I gazed at his small cherubic face, and his eyes lit up, as bright as the sign that brought him so unexpectedly into my life.

Now Layne is a healthy, bouncy three-year-old. The other day my wife and I stopped by for a visit— we're like another set of grandparents to Layne by now—and I couldn't help but think about all those doubts I had once wrestled with.

Does God really hear my prayers? One look into Layne's periwinkle eyes tells me the answer.

A Father's Prayer

by Manuel Hernandez Jr.

—————— ⁄⁄⁄⁄ ——————

*M*anuel . . . Manuel, wake up. The baby's coming." I lifted my head from the pillow and opened my eyes. The dark bedroom slowly came into focus. I could just make out the anxious look on my wife Maria's face. She brought her hands to her round stomach, where our baby girl, Siara, waited to enter the world. "She's ready. I can feel it. Today is the day." I threw off the covers and got dressed. Today is the day, November 27.

Only a year earlier, my son Manuel III had called me while I was at my carpentry job. "Dad, Mom is in the hospital," he said. "They said she had a miscarriage." Maria didn't even know she was pregnant. That made it all the more devastating. We had three teenagers, Manuel, Danny and Cherissa, but another child would've been a blessing.

Maria spent hours praying to find some way to move on. Our pastor, our relatives and friends made us meals, helped take care of our kids and sent their prayers. A community of faith got us through. Just like it had when I was a boy.

We lived in Los Angeles, moving from one bad neighborhood to the next. Both my parents had problems with drugs and alcohol. But things began to change when I was fourteen. My mother was sentenced to a live-in Christian rehabilitation program in Hemet, California. Living there, I learned about faith. These people believed my mother could be helped. They believed I had a future.

I met Maria in Hemet, at a neighbor's Quinceañera, a coming-of-age celebration for a girl's fifteenth birthday. Maria stayed with me despite the mistakes I made over the years. Because of the way I grew up, I didn't know how to be a husband, how to be a father and how to live a life. But once I trusted God to show me, He didn't steer me wrong. I had faith that He would find some way to replace our loss.

When we learned Maria was pregnant again after the miscarriage, we were overjoyed, but cautious. Maria is a diabetic, so she was on a strictly controlled diet. The doctors planned to induce labor. I had walkie-talkies so we would be able to communicate with the kids from the delivery room. At Maria's baby shower all of her friends said blessings over the baby.

It took us six minutes to get to the hospital. "Her contractions are still far apart," the nurse said. "We have time." They admitted Maria to the labor room and our kids took turns visiting her.

The contractions came more frequently. Maria grimaced with each one. "I can feel her moving inside of me." They wheeled her into the delivery room.

"We're going to induce labor," the doctor said. "Now." They broke her water. Suddenly one of the monitors started beeping. The doctor looked up, and the color drained from his face. "Get the crash team," he shouted. Then, "Code Blue!" More nurses rushed into the room. There were about twenty people now, some around the bed, others setting up a table. "Okay, Maria," the doctor said, his voice calm but urgent. "We need you to make this happen now. Push!"

Maria closed her eyes and pushed. A nurse rushed to the doctor's side, pushing a steel cart carrying different instruments. I stared at my wife's face, twisted in pain, her teeth gritted. She was trying so hard. I'm pushing with you, Maria. Push! Finally, I saw my daughter's head poke through. She was blue; she wasn't moving. They pulled her out, cut the umbilical cord and beelined to the table they'd set up. Why isn't she crying? A baby is supposed to cry . . . .

"What's wrong?" Maria cried weakly. The nurse looked at her through tear-filled eyes. "Pray, Maria. Just pray."

The emergency team worked frantically. I heard snippets of clipped replies: "no sign of life," "compressed cord in the birth canal," "no heartbeat." They slid a breathing tube down my tiny daughter's throat. The doctor began gentle compressions on her chest. Never before had I felt so helpless. I unclipped the walkie-talkie from my belt and called Manuel. I tried to steady my shaky voice. "There are some complications with the baby. You must pray."

"I will, Dad," he said. He then told our pastor, who was waiting with him.

I looked at Maria, drenched in sweat. I held her hand lightly and rubbed her shoulder. On the other side of the room, the doctor continued to work. "Zero," a nurse called out, recording the readings off one of the monitors. Maria and I couldn't take our eyes off our daughter. Her hair was dark and curly and wet. "I felt her flutter inside of me," Maria said. "She was alive." The doctor kept at it. A few more minutes ticked by. The nurse checked the vitals once more. "Zero," she said, a flat, hollow sadness to her voice.

The doctor slumped over the table. They removed the breathing tube. The doctor stepped away. "Are you going to call it?" a nurse asked him. He dropped his head. "Yes. We've done all we can."

Maria's face fell. I held her tight. *Lord, no! My wife can't go home without her baby!* All the pain we'd gone through a year ago came flooding back. Most of the staff filed out of the room. Only the doctor and one of the nurses remained.

Suddenly, I was overcome by a strong feeling. An overpowering feeling. Something that was so certain it drove me across the room to the table where Siara lay. I thought about all the prayers we had said. How much God knew we wanted her. No, she could not die.

I went up to my baby and leaned over her. I prayed more intensely than I have in my entire life. *Lord, You have never failed.* I put my hands on Siara. *You raised Lazarus from the dead. Give my daughter Your breath of life.* I kissed Siara on the forehead.

"Would you like to hold her?" the nurse asked Maria. She nodded weakly. The nurse came over and swaddled Siara in a soft blanket then took her over, laid our baby across Maria's chest and backed away.

Maria caressed Siara's tiny face. "Wake up, please," she said. "You have to fight, little one." She took the baby's tiny hand and rubbed it against her own cheek. "God, You have to finish what You started."

Maria wiped away some spittle that had formed on the baby's lips. Then her eyes went wide. "She's breathing!" Maria cried out. My heart jumped. Was it possible?

The nurse shook her head. "No, sweetie," she said sadly. "That's just the oxygen we pumped into her being expelled."

Maria's doctor took his stethoscope and placed it on the baby's chest. "I don't believe it! Call Code Blue again!"

A slight pink began to bloom across Siara's chest. "We're going to take her to the nursery," the doctor said. "We're still working to stabilize her."

Alone in the room, Maria and I cried together. Tears of joy at what we'd just witnessed. The nurses went back and forth to give us updates. "She has a steady heartbeat. She curled her lip and moved her left arm. These are very good signs." I radioed my son in the waiting room the good news and he told our pastor. "She's alive," I said. The praying continued all through that day and that night, until she was out of danger.

With such a traumatic birth, the doctor was worried about brain and heart damage. She suffered some seizures the first days. But her heartbeat was strong and she didn't show any signs of being disabled. On December 8 we finally brought Siara home. An early Christmas present. "I can't explain it," the doctor said. "Siara is a miracle."

Today, when I hold my rosy-cheeked, giggling child in my arms, I realize that Siara is a link in a chain of miracles. From the second we heard the silence where cries should have been, despair threatened to make us give up. That same despair that chased my family from neighborhood to neighborhood growing up. That same despair that hit us after the miscarriage. But like those times and so many more in my life, faith replaced despair with hope. We never lost that hope. And that's a miracle too. The miracle of faith.

AMAZING RECOVERY

by Susan White

I answered my phone at work one morning last October. A call I'd been dreading. "Susan, you need to drive down to the city right away," Mom said. "The doctors don't think your father will make it through the night." My eighty-three-year-old father had slipped on wet leaves near his home in Brooklyn and had hit his head on the sidewalk. He was rushed to the hospital with a fractured skull and brain trauma. The doctors did surgery, but Pop went into seizures and had two severe heart attacks.

I'm a prayer associate for Guideposts Peale Center in Pawling, New York, about seventy-five miles north of New York City. I train volunteers who serve on the phone line and who write prayer responses on our website, OurPrayer.org. I love my job, seeing daily the power of prayer in others' lives. Now I needed to see that power in my life. I sent out an urgent prayer request on the website through my church. Then I drove to the hospital. I found Pop in a coma, his face bruised and swollen, but I hoped somehow he could hear. I whispered in his ear, "Everyone I know is praying for you."

For five days I sat by Pop's side, but there was no change. Any hope he'd come out of the coma grew dim. I knew he was in God's care, but I longed to hear his voice. At the end of the week I had to head home. I bent down and whispered, "Pop, let's pray together." I began the Lord's Prayer. Suddenly Pop's nurse touched my back. I looked up, and she pointed to my father. He was mouthing the words, his lips moving with mine!

Three weeks later I got another call, a happy one. Pop was awake, but confused about what had happened. I filled him in, telling him about everyone praying for him. "I know, Susan," he said. "I could hear them." Pop made a full recovery. Not long ago he took Mom on a trip to Hawaii, leaving me with one more example of the power of prayer.

HEALING CIRCLE

by Virginia Baker

My room at University Hospital in Birmingham, Alabama, was crowded. I gazed up at the faces of my pastor, William Cox, and deacons from our church, including my husband Brooks, who were gathered around my bed.

For more than a year I had been fighting a losing battle against a strange liver ailment, recently lingering in a hepatic coma for three days before coming around. It seemed I had been on the critical list more often than not. But that day I felt relatively good, if weak, and my mind, thankfully, was clear. I caught Brooks's eye and he smiled reassuringly.

Brooks and I attend First Baptist Church in Warrior, Alabama, our hometown, where I am a music teacher. All in all we're a pretty mainstream congregation, and though we certainly believe in prayers for healing, we had never gone in for laying on of hands or anointing with oil. We left that to other churches. But since I had come out of my coma, a verse from the Book of James kept storming into my head: "Is any among you sick? Let them call the elders of the church to pray over them and anoint them with oil in the name of the Lord" (James 5:14 NIV).

I had begun having trouble and a year later was diagnosed with a rare autoimmune disorder that caused my body to attack its own liver cells. In a terrible way, the biological process that was supposed to keep me well was making me sick, deathly sick. By 1986 doctors had all but given up on saving my liver. I had been put at the top of a transplant list at the University of Pittsburgh Medical Center—a pioneer hospital in liver transplants—but no one was sure if a new liver would reverse the disease.

I had heard so many medical opinions that I chose to keep one in the front of my mind at all times, something my internist Dr. Roy Roddam had told me: "Never forget, Virginia, that God is bigger than any disease." You know your condition is serious when your doctor starts reminding you to pray.

My hospital stays had become more frequent and complicated. I suffered weight loss, headaches, extreme fatigue, confusion, jaundice and, especially dangerous, bleeding in my esophagus that sometimes wouldn't stop. My liver functions were deteriorating rapidly. During those three days when I was in a coma, Brooks had stayed by my bedside reading Psalms to me, and our church kept up an unceasing prayer vigil. I came out of it, but in the absence of a miracle I was probably going to die, sooner rather than later, leaving Brooks to raise our three young children without their mother.

With the verse from James echoing in my mind, I had Brooks ask Pastor Cox if he would be willing to try something different—laying on of hands and anointing with oil. "Tell Virginia I don't see why not," he had sent word back, "especially since it's scriptural." And that was why they were gathered in my hospital room that cloudy fall day. I looked at the wreath of faces above me—neighbors, friends, pastor, husband. There was a physical sensation of love pouring from them as they leaned over me—warm, comforting, serene. They had prepared themselves through prayer and fasting, as the Bible instructs. Pastor Cox stood at the head of the bed, with Brooks at my right, and the others completing the circle. Pastor Cox then read James 5:13–14 out loud. Gently, he anointed my forehead with oil. Everyone laid hands on me, tentatively at first. I felt the slight press of fingers and a rippling warmth. I can't say I experienced anything out of the ordinary, save for a subtle yet pervasive sensation of peace that trickled through my entire being. They finished quickly, since I could not have visitors for very long. Holding my husband's hand, I fell into a long, deep sleep.

The next morning my liver specialist, Dr. Colin Helman, performed yet another grueling endoscopic exam of my esophagus and stomach, looking through a long fiber-optic tube to locate blood vessels in danger of rupturing. I was quite surprised to see a pleased but puzzled expression on his face when he finished, and nearly dumbfounded when he said I showed an amazing amount of improvement in the short time since the last endoscopy. He said it as if he had trouble believing it himself. "Virginia," he remarked, "all I can say is that I am very relieved."

I was stunned to hear such good news when all I had been told of late was to expect the worst.

Later, blood work confirmed the unexpected turn in my condition. Doctors and nurses beamed when they came into my room. People once again spoke louder than a whisper. Within days I was removed from the top of the list in Pittsburgh for an urgent liver transplant and put toward the end of the line.

When I was released from the hospital I had an odd, insistent feeling that it was for good. Strength returned; I could eat again; there were no more major bleeding episodes. Over the months my liver-function tests improved steadily. I felt better than I had in a very long time. There was no clear medical explanation for my sudden transformation.

One Sunday about a year later we celebrated the baptism of my youngest son. Pastor Cox led the ceremony and I played piano. Halfway through, a parishioner raced up to me with the message that I had an urgent phone call. I knew what it probably was and quickly followed her to the church office. As I thought, it was the transplant coordinator at the University of Pittsburgh Medical Center. They had a liver for me.

Not long before, I wouldn't have hesitated. Like many transplant candidates, I would have had a bag packed, ready to go at a moment's notice. Now I paused. I had already turned down two earlier transplant opportunities, not yet ready to face the overwhelming ordeal of surgery. This was probably going to be my final opportunity. But if my liver was slowly healing, as it surely appeared to be, might someone else need a transplant more urgently than I? Should I step aside and trust the Lord?

I told the hospital I would call back in ten minutes, and sent the parishioner for Brooks, Pastor Cox and Dr. Oliver Harper, our family physician, who was attending our son's baptism. "What do I do?" I asked them, not so much afraid as anxious to make a quick decision.

Brooks covered my hand with his and all at once an almost physical memory of that day in my hospital room came rushing back. I could see the faces above me and feel the faint warmth of fingertips through the thin, crisp sheet. In an instant I knew I wanted to remove myself from the transplant list. My healing was well under way. Why interfere? "What would you advise if I were your wife?" I asked Dr. Harper.

"I'd tell you not to have it."

That was all I needed to hear. I called the hospital and told them I wouldn't be having the surgery. Then I returned to my son's baptism and took my seat at the piano as the service resumed.

Today I am the mother of three children, ages twenty-two, nineteen and sixteen. As I've said, I come from a fairly traditional church background. I don't use the word *miracle* lightly. Yet what else can I call it? I was in and out of a coma, my life hanging by a thread. I was told my liver was beyond saving, and even with a new one I would be fighting heavy odds. So how do I explain that years later, after six inexperienced members of my church stood in a circle, laid their hands on me and asked the Lord for a healing, my liver functions better than doctors ever dreamed it would and that I enjoy good health again?

No, I don't use the word *miracle* lightly. Yet when I look back on my experience I find no other word that fits, no other concept that makes sense. The Lord's grace shone on me, and for a reason I am not yet meant to understand fully, I was allowed to live. God showed that He is bigger than any disease.

3

INCREDIBLE REDEMPTION

*I*n him we have redemption through his blood, the forgiveness of our trespasses, according to the riches of his grace.

EPHESIANS 1:7 ESV

*Omnipotent God, Your power to change lives is incredible.
No "case" is hopeless, no prodigal too far gone for You to save
when lifted to You in prayer. Thank You for Your grace
and mercy and redemption!*

My Little Lamb

by Luanne Bandy Holzloehner

————— ∿ —————

I pulled the barn door closed behind me, shutting out the bitter January cold and swirling snow. The ewe was on the floor of her stall, her head resting on a patch of straw. I stared at her swollen belly. What a time to give birth, I thought.

Her flanks heaved. Any time now. I saw the strain in her eyes and reached down to stroke her side. She snapped at my hand. I pulled back. What ever made Henry and me think we could raise sheep? I wondered. Or do any of this—build a log house, grow our own food, keep livestock for milk and eggs?

I was a city girl, but I'd always dreamed of moving to the country and living off the land. God's land. After my kids were grown, Henry and I got married— a second marriage for both—and we'd decided to start a second life too. We had given up the rat race, our daily commutes, our nine-to-five jobs. We had moved close to nature. We sold our city homes and bought five acres in Vermont dairy country. Our first night there I hugged Henry tightly and told him, "Our lives will be wonderful now."

We found a little white clapboard church that we liked, and dutifully introduced ourselves to our neighbors. I got a part-time job at a school and Henry took a job delivering newspapers, but mostly we stuck to ourselves and tried to make the farm work. Wasn't that the idea? To be far from civilization. To be independent. To live close to the land and the few sheep and cows we raised. Yet from the very beginning, it had been a struggle to survive. A lonely struggle.

I stared at the ewe, struggling herself now. *Lord, I thought this move would bring us closer to You. Why do You feel so far away?* I prayed.

I tossed a handful of fresh hay into the ewe's stall. It was all I could do for her right now. Then I stepped out the barn door, threw my weight against it to shut it and headed through the fierce wind to the house. I would check on her again after dinner.

Each day, it seemed, brought a new problem. One day our pickup rolled down the hill and plunged into the pond. Not long after, the tractor we used as a snowplow broke down and we had to fight a half-mile through ice and hip-deep snow just to reach the end of our driveway. Then our well ran dry. The workers kept drilling deeper and deeper into the ground looking for water, each foot costing precious dollars we didn't have.

Maybe this life was a terrible mistake, I thought, trudging through the snow. The work was endless. *Maybe we should go back and live in the city again.* At least that was something we knew. When something went wrong I could look in the yellow pages and make a call. Or if I ran out of something, I could knock on my next-door neighbor's door or run to the corner market. What were you supposed to do in the country at the end of a dirt road without a neighbor in sight?

Henry and I ate dinner in near silence. We did the dishes, then I pulled on Henry's heavy jacket and headed back to the barn. Inside, everything was still. My clouds of cold breath hung in the air. I peeked over the side of the stall. There, nestled in the matted hay, were two tiny balls of wool. Twins.

"You did it," I said to the ewe. I wanted to celebrate with her. But I saw in her eyes that something was wrong.

One of the babies was curled up, motionless, in the corner. Dead?

I bent over and picked it up. The lamb wriggled slightly in my arms. Relief washed over me. I carried it to its mother. "Help your baby," I urged her. But the ewe just pushed it aside. She had already given up on its survival. If the baby were to survive, it would be up to me.

One more hopeless thing, I thought. Still, how could I not try?

I tucked the tiny ball of fur beneath Henry's coat and carried her to our cabin. Henry quickly helped me arrange a little playpen with hay. Above it we placed a heat lamp to keep her warm. I decided to name her Lorrie.

For a week I looked after her constantly. Nights, I slept on an old recliner with the lamb snuggled in my lap and fed her every three hours with a baby bottle.

One night, as I cuddled her in my arms, she looked up at me with utter trust. That look unnerved me. *Who am I to save her?* I thought. I could barely save myself.

Please, Lord, save Lorrie, I prayed. *She's so weak and help-less. She needs you so much.* And then more softly I added, *So do I*. I put her down on the floor. She stood for a moment on her wobbly legs. Then she sank weakly back to her knees.

I picked her up again and cuddled her in the chair. I started to doze off. A thought startled me awake. *Take*

Lorrie to church tomorrow. I smiled, shook my head. *Crazy*, I thought to myself. *Take a lamb to church?* I shook my head again and went back to sleep.

The next morning I couldn't get the notion out of my head as I dressed for church. When I passed Lorrie on my way toward the door I grabbed her from her playpen. I wrapped her in a soft blue blanket and headed out to the pickup. Henry was waiting for me behind the wheel. He looked at me in disbelief.

"What are you doing with her?" he asked me.

"I'm bringing Lorrie with us," I told him quietly.

Henry started to protest, then just shook his head and helped us in.

We pulled up to the church and climbed out of the pickup truck. I took a deep breath, then walked to the entrance with Lorrie in my arms. The minister stood in the doorway, greeting parishioners.

"I'd like to say a few words after the service, if it's okay," I said to him.

He spotted the little lamb, curled up in the blanket. He raised his eyebrows, surprised, then nodded that it was okay.

I led Henry to a back pew. At the end of the service, I walked to the altar, hiding Lorrie from view. Then I turned to the congregation and unwrapped the blanket. People stared and murmured when they saw Lorrie.

I wasn't sure what I wanted to say. But deep inside I knew I had to do this. I set Lorrie down on her wobbly limbs. As she struggled to walk, I explained how important it had become for me that she survive. And then the words just spilled out.

"I thought life would be easy here, that I could make it on my own. But I am weak and helpless. Sometimes I feel like there isn't any help. Then I try to remember, 'The Lord is my shepherd and I shall not want...'" My voice trailed off. Henry stood at the back of the church, his cap in his hand, blinking back tears.

Silence.

I picked Lorrie up, lowered my head to hide my face and headed quickly toward the door. But before I could reach it the congregation was on their feet, closing in around me.

A little girl's hand reached out to pet Lorrie. A woman's arm tightened around my shoulders. Then another and another until it felt like the whole church was holding me, holding me the way I held that little lamb, the way the Lord would always hold me closer and closer.

At last I had found what I had been seeking all along.

THE YELLOW KITE

by Beverly Newman

———〰———

I stood at the window and watched the neighborhood children flying their kites on the hill behind our house. My four-year-old son Michael stood next to me with his face eagerly pressed against the glass. Then, looking up at me with pleading eyes, he again asked if he could have a kite like the other children.

For days now, ever since he had first seen them congregate on the hill, Michael had been asking the same question, and had been given the same answer: "Wait until you are a little older."

It was easier not to go into a long explanation, but actually Michael was too young to fly a kite all by himself, and that meant that one of us would always have to go with him to help. Because of my health I simply didn't have the strength or energy, and my husband was usually at work. Once again, Michael hid his face in my skirt, something he always did when he was going to cry and didn't want me to see.

As I turned from the window, I felt like crying myself. I looked around the room; the furniture was shabby and worn, and the walls were badly in need of paint. You could see the light places on them, the spots where previous tenants had hung their pictures. Even though we had lived here for several months, I had not done very much to fix the place up. We had moved so many times, and each time it seemed like the neighborhood was a little more run-down, and the house a little older, each one in need of repairs.

My husband Bill worked long, irregular hours at his job and earned a good salary. However, there was never enough money and we kept going deeper in debt. I had lost three children through miscarriages and the complications that followed caused me to make several emergency trips to the hospital and to be constantly under a doctor's care. As a result, a tension had grown between us and we found we could no longer get along with one another.

It all looked so hopeless; even God seemed to have forgotten us. I prayed so often about our problems, asking God for help, but things only seemed to get worse. I found myself thinking, *God doesn't care, and I guess I don't either.*

I walked over to the mirror and studied my reflection. It was almost like looking at a stranger. I looked pale and worn, much older than my years. I no longer bothered to fix my face or do anything with my hair. I stepped back and studied my whole image—the old dress that I had worn all week was wrinkled and torn at the pocket and there was a button missing at the neck.

As I stood there and stared at myself, a feeling of dread, almost panic, came over me, and it filled my whole body with fear. It was the realization that I was giving up on life. I had stopped caring about anything; I felt defeated. I could no longer rise above the depression that had taken hold of me.

In the last few months, my husband had grown rather quiet and we did not talk much. I was aware of his eyes studying me when he thought I was preoccupied with something. I used to be so particular about everything. Bill had not said a word about the change that had come over me, but his actions said a lot. He made a special effort to get me interested in new things, but I did not respond. In fact, I did not respond to him in any way, and he did not know quite how to handle me anymore.

Michael was the one spark of life left for me. He could make me smile, and when he hugged me, I would feel love. I clung to him much in the way one would cling to a life preserver. He needed me and I knew it—that kept me going.

As I tucked him into bed that evening, Michael said, "Mommy, may I pray to God to send me a yellow kite?" Then, fearing that I might again repeat what I had said so many times before, he added, "Maybe He doesn't think I'm too young."

"Yes," I said. "We will leave it up to Him to decide about it once and for all." I was tired of the whole thing and hoped that maybe this would make Michael stop talking about it.

Michael prayed his prayer and fell asleep with a smile on his face. As I stood there looking down at that beautiful child with the blond curls, so trusting in his faith that God would answer his little prayer, I found myself questioning God. Would He really answer such a small prayer when He had chosen not to hear any of my frantic pleas or send me any help to relieve my situation? "Oh, God," I prayed, "please help me! Show me the way out of this dark place."

The next morning as I raised the shade in the kitchen, I stared at the sight that met my eyes—a string hanging down in front of the window. Not quite able to believe the thoughts that were being put together in my mind, I found myself running out the back door and into the yard. There it was, a yellow kite, caught on the roof with its string hanging down.

"Oh, thank You, God, thank You!" I repeated over and over again. I was thanking Him for the yellow kite, and I was thanking Him for the joy that was flooding into my soul. He had answered the prayer of a little boy, just a little prayer, but by answering that prayer, He had also answered my prayer for help.

Suddenly I remembered Michael. I ran to his room, scooped him up in my arms and carried him into the backyard. He was still half-asleep and didn't quite know what to make of this mother who was babbling about something on the roof and saying, "Wait until you see!"

He clapped his hands and bounced up and down in my arms when he saw the kite. "Mommy, Mommy, and it's even yellow!" he exclaimed. I smiled at him and added, "It's a miracle too." He hugged me and said, "I knew God would answer my prayer. I just knew He would."

I thought to myself, This was why I had been so depressed. I had lost my faith. I had turned my back on God, and then insisted that He had stopped caring. The yellow kite was not the only miracle that God sent to us that morning.

When Bill came home we took the kite to the beach and flew it. It went so high that it was almost out of sight for a while. Bill said he had never seen a kite fly as high. We asked all over the neighborhood but we never found a trace of the kite's former owner.

We moved several times in the years that followed, and the yellow kite always went with us. My depression left me and as my health improved, so did my relationship with my husband.

At each new place I would hang the kite in some corner where I could see it as I went about my duties. It served as a reminder that no matter how bad things may seem, we must never lose sight of the fact that God cares, that He hears our prayers. No request is too big or too small to bring before Him.

A New Look at Myself

by Dorothy Hopkins

———————— ·ᗯ· ————————

Just before the Christmas season one year, my situation seemed impossible, or so I thought. I had a dull job with poor pay and a despot for a boss; my dreary basement apartment, in Chicago, was shared with what I considered an ungrateful, unemployed sister; my ten-year-old daughter was beginning to show signs of being mentally challenged; my estranged husband completely ignored his obligations. I felt hopeless.

During the long, daily ride to work on the streetcar, I had developed a sort of mechanical habit of praying, as though God were a Santa Claus. I would pray for a raise in salary, but I hated my job and my boss. I would pray for help from my estranged husband, but I considered him a cheat, a liar and a drunkard. I would pray for better living conditions, but I despised our apartment and monotonous "economical" food.

Then, on the very Friday before Christmas, the sky fell in! I lost my purse containing a week's salary! I was in a department store when I became aware that my purse was gone. It was closing time and I had to rush to the office to report my loss, and to ask for carfare home.

Outside, on State Street, Christmas carols filled the air, but their beauty did not penetrate the bitterness in my heart. At that moment I felt that Jesus Christ's mission on Earth was all in vain.

By the time I got a seat on the streetcar, anger commenced to dissolve into self-pity. I began to pray again. "Why, God," I asked, "why did all these things have to happen to me?" Tears came to my eyes, and I had no handkerchief. I felt alone in a world without love.

Presently I felt something touch my hand. A woman sitting next to me was silently offering a handful of tissues. She didn't speak, and neither did I, but somehow I knew that she was also handing me compassion and understanding. Suddenly a wall seemed to give way inside of me and I felt ashamed.

I began to pray again, but this time with real humility. I prayed for forgiveness; I prayed for guidance; I prayed for understanding. And as I prayed an amazing transformation took place in my attitude concerning the people toward whom I had felt so bitter earlier: my sister suddenly was an undeserving captive of my sharp criticism and morose outlook. I began to wonder if the relationship between my husband and myself might not have been different had I given more thought to his viewpoints, and less to my own problems.

For the first time, I began to associate my boss's disagreeableness with his struggle to keep the firm solvent against stiff competition. And for the first time in many months I thought of my daughter as someone sweet, to be loved and cared for, rather than a constant source of worry and anxiety.

By the time I arrived home, being broke no longer seemed so important. I still had a job, a family to love and to love me, and a warm apartment. Many, many had less!

Next morning a surprising succession of blessings started to reach us. First, two young school girls delivered a large Christmas box of food. Soon after that our insurance agent came by with word that I could convert my policy and receive a sizable cash settlement.

Also, in the next few days, I received a money order from my husband, and my unemployed sister secured work during the holidays.

To top it all, on the first of the year I was promoted to a much better job with a raise. My employer had been considering me for the promotion, but before my change hadn't liked my negative attitude toward work.

Although this whole experience seemed to bring many material rewards, the most important to me was discovering the kind of prayer where I quit trying to run my life and turned everything over to God. The result was that God gave me the desire to change myself and at the same time allowed me to view through His loving eyes all the wonderful people close to me.

CHAIN REACTION

by Randy Long

— ·················· ~ㅠ~ ··················—

I had always been skeptical about prayer. What good did it do? Three years ago I found out.

I was shopping at a local drugstore when all of a sudden I felt disoriented and unsteady. An employee noticed. He sat me down right away, then managed to get in touch with my wife Jo Ann. She came to pick me up and, at the pharmacist's urging, took me to the emergency room.

In the car I couldn't buckle my seatbelt. It seemed as if my fingers just wouldn't work. By the time we got to the hospital, I couldn't even have told you what day it was. Tests were inconclusive. The doctor decided to keep me overnight for observation. By the next morning I was having convulsions. They moved me to the intensive care unit, where I fell into a coma.

The doctors told my wife the prognosis wasn't good. I had the West Nile virus; it was affecting my brain and nervous system. They'd do what they could, but there was no specific treatment known to fight the infection.

Maybe the doctors couldn't do anything, but Jo Ann could. She prayed. She also told her sister, Judy, about my condition. Judy organized a citywide prayer chain. On September 19 everyone in Selma was asked to pray for me between 7:00 PM and 8:00 PM. They prayed that night. And the next. And the next. After three weeks, I finally came out of the coma. I had no idea how long I'd been out or what was wrong with me. "What happened?"

"You have the West Nile virus," Jo Ann told me.

"Is it serious?"

"Randy, you've been in a coma. The doctors told us it would take a miracle to bring you back."

That it did. I am back. Not just healthy, but a changed man. Thanks to the good people of Selma, I'm no longer a skeptic.

A Chance to Forgive

by Frances McGee-Cromartie

--------------------------- ·⁓· ---------------------------

Thursday. My turn to pick up doughnuts for the Montgomery County Prosecutor's office, where I work. I was in a rush, as usual, but it wouldn't take long to swing by my favorite bakery. It was good to see so much activity on a gray February morning: kids holding their parents' hands as they walked to school, folks hurrying to work. But one man stood out. He was pacing in front of the parking lot next to the bakery, wearing a rumpled overcoat and a blue knit hat. His body language made me wary. As a prosecutor, I'm trained to notice these things. I drove past the lot and pulled up on the street, as close to the bakery as I could get.

I quickly paid for my doughnuts and fished my keys from my pocket. I was heading back to my car when I spotted him again. Probably a crackhead, the way he slouched. I picked up my pace. Just then he stepped in front of me. "This is a robbery," he snarled. "Don't make it difficult."

Did he say he's going to rob me? I'd heard it described hundreds of times by victims: time seemed to slow and a feeling of unreality set in. "Hurry up!" he said. He unzipped his coat, revealing an opened switchblade. Yet, I was frozen with shock, a combination of fear, disbelief and anger. Anger that this could happen to me. He reached out and yanked my purse off my arm in a single, violent motion. My keys and the doughnuts tumbled to the pavement.

The mugger pointed the knife, pushing it at me as a warning. Then he sprinted down the alley and through the parking lot, clutching my bag. I let loose a scream that had been building in the few seconds that the mugging occurred. It curdled my own blood. I trembled uncontrollably. Somehow I made it back to the bakery and used their phone to call my husband. "I've been robbed," I managed to gasp. "My purse is gone. Wallet. Everything."

"I'll be right there," he said. "All that matters is that you're okay."

He was right, of course. I was lucky not to get hurt. I've said the same thing to victims. But okay? Certainly not. This time I was the victim. I'd been violated.

The police came and found the robber's coat and hat in a search of the area. There were hairs that could be used for a DNA sample. The next day I skipped work to review hundreds of mug shots at the police station, but I couldn't match my assailant's face to a known felon's. Worse, all those mug shots of all those criminals made me feel vulnerable. I didn't want to be alone. And I felt I could never go back to my favorite little bakery. I lay in bed that night unable to rest. I should have felt secure beside my husband, but my thoughts were trained on the stranger who'd done this terrible thing. Would he come after me? He knew where I lived now that he had my wallet. I closed my eyes and tried to sleep. Impossible. The anger I felt during the attack welled up and I fantasized that I'd fought back. I felt bolder. I visualized myself standing tall in the courtroom at his sentencing, upbraiding this villain for what he'd done to me. I wanted him to pay.

I awoke in the morning still feeling vengeful. I had a right, though, didn't I? I sat down alone at my dining-room table, sipping my coffee. I felt rage overtaking me, and I didn't like it. I needed to pray. *God, I know You protected me from the mugger's knife. Now protect me from my hateful feelings.* In the stillness of the room, an answer came. *Have the church pray for the robber.*

Pray for him? The criminal? That wasn't what I expected. Yet throughout the day the thought kept popping up. Finally I dialed my pastor's number. I was indignant as I told Father Ben what had happened. "Pray for my attacker!" I said. "That's crazy, right?"

"Maybe not," Father Ben said. "Just make sure to come to church tomorrow."

The next morning during the service, Father Ben stood in front of the altar. "Please join me, Frances," he said. The surprise must have been plain on my face. I rose hesitantly and walked down the aisle till I reached his side. "Frances was mugged on Thursday in an act of terrible violence," he announced. There was a collective gasp. "Let us give thanks for her deliverance from harm." Heads bowed and whispered prayers filled the sanctuary. Next, Father Ben asked us all to pray once more. This time, incredibly, for the robber. "Release him from his dependence on drugs, Lord," he said. "Show him Your way. The way to You. The way to forgiveness."

"Your way," I repeated. My way was vengeance. I certainly had a right to be upset, even angry. I had a right to demand justice. But I also needed to let it all go, to let God. I closed my eyes and prayed with my whole being. I would not meet evil with evil. *Show him the way to forgiveness*, I repeated, and laid my fears and anger at the foot of the cross.

When I returned to work on Monday each of my coworkers stopped by to see me. The support felt good, but things weren't right yet. There was one thing I had to conquer. "I'll bring the doughnuts tomorrow," I announced on Wednesday afternoon. "Thursday's my day."

"Where are you gonna get them?" a colleague asked, furrowing her brow.

"Same place," I said.

Thursday morning I retraced the steps I'd taken a week earlier. I parked in the same spot, went into the bakery and strode back out minutes later with a box of Dayton's best doughnuts. My coworkers cheered as I carried the box into the office like a trophy. Scared? Yeah, a little bit. I'd learned that there are things out there we need to be scared of, and more so that the Lord protects us from harm not only from others but from our own feelings.

More than a year has passed and my robber hasn't been apprehended. I still ask God to direct his life and deliver him from the forces making him cause pain to others. Of course I still hope he'll be caught. When he is, I hope he'll know he's been given a chance to change. When God gives you a chance, you take it. I know. After all, He gave me one: a chance to forgive.

OPENED EYES

Cheryl Pietromonaco

────── ⁓⁓⁓ ──────

One thing troubled me about my husband: he didn't believe in God. "Believe what you like," he said, "but there isn't someone up there making miracles happen." I prayed hard for him to come around. That would definitely take a miracle.

One winter we took a vacation in the Montana mountains. His brother owned a cabin there and lent us his Jeep—"You'll need the four-wheel drive," he said. He handed us a large key ring, indicating the key for the Jeep and the one for the cabin. We arrived late in the afternoon. I was awed by the isolation, the delicate, powdery snow frosting everything in sight and the utter silence. We dropped our bags, took off our coats and my husband tossed the keys onto the kitchen table. They landed with a metallic clank. I needed a drink, but there was no running water. "Let's grab a bucket; we'll get some water from the creek," my husband said. We left the door open to clear the musty air while we were out.

We weren't far when a strong gust of wind blew. There was a loud bang. The cabin door! We stopped and stared at each other, thinking the same thing, I hope that door didn't just lock.... We ran back through the snow. The door was locked tight. "The keys are on the kitchen table!" my husband groaned.

He rammed a shoulder against the door. It didn't budge. "See if there's a wire or something in the Jeep," he told me. "Maybe we can pick the lock."

"I'll say a prayer too," I told him.

Nothing of help was in the glove compartment or seat pockets. I searched and prayed. Under the driver's seat I felt something and fished it out. A ring of keys! Just like the set my brother-in-law gave us. I rushed back to the cabin. Sure enough, one of the keys opened the door. Saved!

My husband looked at the table. The keys he'd tossed on it were gone! We looked for that first ring of keys, but never found another set.

Later, my brother-in-law insisted the key ring he'd handed us was the only set he had. "I just don't get it," my husband said, confused. But I did. I got the miracle I'd asked for.

The cabin door wasn't the only thing opened up that day. My husband's eyes finally started to open as well.

ONE SCALY GODSEND

by Chana Keefer

Mom! Look what I found!" Micah ran across the park, cupping something in his palm. "She ran across the grass, right up to me!" He grinned at the scaly green thing in his palm. "She likes me. Can I keep her?"

Ugh. I wasn't crazy about a lizard in my house. But lately my twelve-year-old needed every friend he could get. He hated school. He picked on his little brother and sisters. He screamed and yelled at anyone who crossed him—especially me. I'd prayed like crazy: *God, show me how to reach him. I'll do whatever it takes.* Still, things had gotten worse, and I was worried—no, scared. It was like living with a time bomb. If Micah was like this at twelve, what lay ahead for our family when he was a teenager?

If I nixed the lizard, we'd have another blowup. Yes, it might mean more trouble later on if I had to nag Micah to take care of his pet. (In fact, who knew how to take care of a lizard?) In the end, the happiness I saw on Micah's face as he stroked the creature gently with his finger sold me. "She—he—it—whatever, is going to be your responsibility, Micah."

"Awesome!" he practically shouted. "Wanna hold her?" Not really. But I let him put the lizard in my hand. *Lord, please don't let this be one more thing that separates us.*

Micah read everything he could find about lizard care. "Bettie" went everywhere with him, perched on his shoulder or snuggled under his hat. People stopped Micah on the street to ask questions: "What kind of lizard is it?" "What do you feed it?"

You know something? All that attention made Micah more outgoing. Less hostile. His attitude about school and his behavior improved. I never had to nag him to care for Bettie, and the tenderness he showed her spilled over to the way he treated others, and me. I stopped bracing myself for the next battle.

Today, Micah is a teenager. Reptiles have become his passion—he even has three snakes now. It took some getting used to. But then I remembered my desperate prayer and my promise to do whatever it took. Like so many answered prayers, what it took was what I never could have imagined.

TUESDAYS WITH MARY

by Mary Snorek

I loved being a music teacher, loved getting kids excited about singing. Except on Tuesdays. Or at least on Tuesdays the year I had a class of third graders who had no interest in music. I went out of my way to find songs about sports, the outdoors, things they liked. I even played games with them. The kids just didn't care. They goofed off. When I coaxed them to sing, they'd whine, "Do we have to?" It got so I'd lay awake on Mondays, wondering why I couldn't get through to the kids. *Maybe I should call in sick tomorrow so I won't have to face them,* I thought one sleepless night. Then a thought entered my mind, *Pray for them.*

Ha! Lot of good that would do. But the idea wouldn't go away. So I pictured the class. There was the blonde girl in the front row whose parents were divorcing. The freckle-faced boy in the next row whose dad had lost his job. I'd forgotten how many of the kids were going through hard times. Seat by seat, I prayed for each student. Then I went sound to sleep.

Tuesday morning I didn't feel stressed, though I heard the third graders making a ruckus in the hall. I was relaxed and smiling. They came in and went to their seats . . . so quietly I could hardly believe it. "Let's sing 'The Farmer in the Dell,'" I said. Not a single complaint. The class sang with gusto. Were these the same kids I'd been struggling with? I decided to push the limits. "Who wants to play a music game?" Hands shot up. "Me" "Me too!" Before I knew it, class was over. I got a lot of smiles as the kids filed out. "That was fun," the boy with freckles said. "See you next Tuesday, Mrs. Snorek."

"I can't wait," I said. I meant it.

No, the kids hadn't changed, but their teacher certainly had.

To Tame a Whirlwind

by Corinne Diller

⸺•⸺

The Lord's Prayer had always been a part of my life, since I was a child. But one afternoon on a camping vacation with my husband John and our daughter Becky, I found myself meditating on one phrase, "Thy will be done...." *Thy will be done.* I didn't know why that phrase stuck in my mind that September afternoon. I did know that I usually did God's will only when it was convenient.

So, sitting there, swatting at flies in that marshy campground, miles away from anything, I said, "Okay, Lord, Thy will be done, even if it's not convenient."

I don't know what made me do that either. I guess I felt I ought to. But it didn't take God long to respond.

When we returned home, I got a phone call. It was the social worker John and I had been talking to about adopting a child: "There's a little four-year-old girl in need of a home. She comes from a background of abuse. She's quite a handful, but while in foster care this past year, she was toilet trained. And she can dress herself, a little."

John and I went down to the office to read through Shelly's records. We were shocked: beaten repeatedly by parents, malnourished, epileptic, amblyopic, ruptured eardrums, severely mentally challenged, hyperactive, prognosis for survival—fair.

A letter from a psychotherapist caught our attention, especially his recommendation: "Shelly should be placed in a safe room where she cannot harm herself, and be made as comfortable as possible. I see no other possibilities for her."

Dear Lord, I thought, *can taking on this child really be Your will?*

I shuddered at what God had come up with. But I knew He wanted this desolate child to have a family. And He wanted that family to be us! Perhaps that is why the red tape of adoption went so rapidly.

We met Shelly on the run. We caught a glimpse of her as she raced by, a huge purplish birthmark covering half her face, both blue eyes squinting, and stringy, honey-colored hair flying behind. She couldn't sit still, she couldn't talk, and we weren't even sure that she could see us very well. We were just large shadowy figures, strangers trying to say friendly things to a little girl whose ears were infected and filled with fluid.

Her first day home, Shelly ran and screamed hour after hour. She could not seem to sit still.

"Shelly, come on and have lunch with us," I coaxed her as she streaked past. She never paused, just kept going. She didn't even look at us.

Toys went flying, books came off shelves as fast as her little hands could grab them. Becky, almost five, let out a tearful yell as her new sister punched and pinched her way through that day.

Then, when I opened the refrigerator door, Shelly yanked out some stale macaroni. I raced after her, yelling, "John, catch her—that stuff is moldy!"

Shelly flitted around furniture, in and out of rooms, as she jammed the hard concoction into her mouth. Finally I cornered her in the living room, and as I removed that awful stuff from her mouth, her teeth clamped down on my fingers.

She was an octopus of arms and legs, hitting and kicking and screaming incoherent sounds. John and Becky and I got some bruises that first week, but it didn't matter too much. We'd already begun loving Shelly.

We knew the past that Shelly would have to overcome—her first three years had been spent in one room. A bowl of food had been set on the floor for her—when anyone came home to her. So effectively did she shut out the world that had hurt her that she didn't cry even when spanked, nor laugh when tickled. And she didn't want us to breach that barrier.

We knew the difficulties she faced in fitting into a different lifestyle—one that took her out to school, to the zoo, the beach, stores; one filled with ever-present parents, sister, pets, neighbors; one that made tremendous demands on her to conform to new ways.

Could she do it? Professionals had said, "She can't." She was a bundle of nerves and bones who probably wouldn't live very long. "Don't bother..." they suggested.

And yet, that phrase "Thy will be done" kept coming to me. God had a purpose in all of this. He had brought us together. He must know something the professionals didn't.

I sat looking at Shelly in those early days and told myself, "Either I'm going to spend the rest of my life apologizing for Shelly's behavior, or I'm going to help her learn how to act." I gritted my teeth and chose the latter course... and asked God to help.

After that there were days upon days of capturing Shelly just to talk to her, forcing her to look at us when we spoke to her. Night after night of lying on a cot in her room and repeating over and over again, "Lie down, Shelly...lie down...lie down." She hit us when we hugged her, stole toys from other children, got into fights and ate more food than she could hold because she feared that there wouldn't be more, like in the bad old days.

For the first weeks we had to hide all the food in the house. We kept coming at Shelly with incredible demands: "Sit in the chair at the table; pick up your toys; shut the door!" Things we'd been told that she'd never understand. She went everywhere that John and Becky and I went. She had to get used to new clothes, different foods, even a new name.

She had to get used to church, to sitting still through services, to waiting for grace before meals. She had to get used to a classroom full of noisy children.

"Would it be all right to tie her in her chair?" the teacher wanted to know.

"No," we replied. "She can learn. Give her a little more time."

Shelly had a history of running away. She tried it the first time we visited the zoo. We sat near the bears' cage and watched those huge shaggy creatures lumber around, while Shelly made off down the path. But as she ran along, we noticed, she looked over her shoulder to see if we were following. We weren't.

"Shelly, come back and watch the bears with us," we all said. Soon, discovering that it was no fun to run away when no one was running after her, she was back with us pointing at the bears.

And as those first weeks became her first months with us, she discovered other things. When you pick up your toys without being asked, you get an extra hug. When you sit through an entire meal without running from the table, you get an outpouring of cheers from Mommy and Daddy and Becky. And, yes, it's okay to close your eyes during grace—nothing bad will happen to you. If you fight with Becky over a toy, neither you nor Becky gets to play with it.

Soon there was less pinching and punching. After a while, Shelly began sleeping through the night. And her teacher no longer asked to tie her in a chair!

Somehow, we felt, God's will was developing, evolving, in this child Shelly, who even let us hug her. She wasn't hugging back, though.

Testing showed that Shelly was allergic to all kinds of chemical food additives—as well as to perfume, chlorine, dye, paint, cleaning fluids, bug sprays, detergents and the glue used in laying linoleum. Even the food coloring in children's Tylenol made her sick.

In the past years Shelly had been on thirty different drugs, some of them with dangerous side effects. These had been prescribed by doctors who had never tested her—simply kept prescribing medication. When tested, Shelly showed no trace of epilepsy. It is thought that the drugs themselves caused epileptic episodes. Most weren't even supposed to be taken by children.

"You want a glass of milk, Shelly?" I would ask. Shelly reached for the glass. "Say milk, Shelly...milk...milk." Shelly stuck out her lip petulantly.

"Come on, Shelly, now try...milk," I'd say encouragingly.

She looked at me in frustration, her weak little eyes beginning to spill over.

"Now, Shelly, just give it a try. I know you can say it. Just try...milk."

"Mik." She struggled to form the word. I barely understood it, but what a thrill. She was trying! Thank God, she was trying. And, oh, she got a big hug along with that glass of milk.

And, after that, "cat," "dog," "toy" came tumbling out with much toil and inaccuracy. It is extremely difficult for people with hearing problems to pronounce words correctly. In Shelly's case it was thought she'd never be able to talk at all. But God knew better.

In December Shelly went to the eye doctor. It took an hour and a half of holding a restless Shelly on my lap, but the examination showed that Shelly had astigmatism in both eyes. She had to wear a patch and a pair of glasses over the eye with amblyopia. She, of course, didn't want to keep them on. "She'll never be able to do it," we were told. But we insisted. And she finally did.

Then, incredibly, miraculously, she began watching TV. And then coloring. And looking at picture books. "Thy will be done," I said silently to God.

Shelly began drawing squares and circles for the first time. She began naming a few letters in the alphabet, telling animals apart. "Cow," she'd say, as we sat together reading. Sure enough, it was a picture of a cow she was pointing to.

The amblyopic eye began working in unison with the stronger eye, and Shelly began to look at us when we talked to her. Small accomplishments for any other child, for her these were victories.

At Christmas, Grandma came to visit and to lavish attention on the girls. What a special time for all of us, especially Shelly, who had acquired a fondness for hugs.

After Grandma left, Shelly grew thoughtful. Then she asked me, "Like Grandma?" There was a short pause, then she continued, "Like Mommy? Like Daddy? Like Becky?" She was asking if it was all right to open up to us. It was the first time we knew that she cared about us. We all clamored to hug her, and there was a slight, ever-so-slight squeeze back. But still no smile came to those serious blue eyes or that pursed little mouth.

Then, one Saturday afternoon in January, the four of us sat in the Dairy Queen huddled over ice-cream sodas and orange juice. Suddenly a blast of air from the ceiling fan sent a paper napkin scooting across the table and to the floor. Shelly's face lit up and we heard a tiny giggle. We could hardly believe our ears! We made the napkin repeat its silly table-top swoosh, and this time we all giggled; we laughed out of sheer delight that all of us could laugh together now. How good to see that God's will was being done!

Right before she came to us, Shelly's ears were surgically drained; and she took antibiotics and anti-histamines daily to prevent the fluids from returning. Gradually her hearing improved so that she could hear voices in the next room, a dog barking down the street, a knock on the door. She began speaking more—"Oh, loud noise! Hurt my ear!"

A year and a half later we had a healthy little Shelly. Tests showed her brain waves and skull X-rays to be normal. When she was four, her test scores at school placed her at the two-year-old level. When she turned five, she was scoring at age-level four. In just a few months she had made enormous gains.

Her birthmark was removed by plastic surgery. There was no damage to veins or muscles, which is sometimes the case with such a mark. Today she sees, she hears, she laughs, she sings, she talks a mile a minute. Day by day her enthusiasm for life grows.

And day by day she proves to us that God's will is being done.

WHO'LL START THE RAIN?

by Wanda Rosseland

—⁂—

It's too dry for June 1. For the third year in a row, drought conditions were parching Montana. I could feel the relentless heat on my face and arms as I headed across the farmyard to the house.

Earlier in the spring when we took the cows to grass, instead of new crested wheat greening the hills and creek bottoms, brittle brown stems from last year crunched under the cows' hooves. Normally, snowpack in the mountains fed the rivers through the summer, but now the rivers were nothing more than useless shallow streams.

Inside I spoke to my friend Jeanie on the phone. "What can we do about this drought?" I asked.

"Wanda, you're good with words. Write a prayer to send out. Something to get everyone praying."

I can't do that, I thought. But then I sat down at my computer and began to type: "We need to pray for rain to fall across our state of Montana." The words flowed. "Soft, gentle rain over our mountains, steady, even rain moving across our prairies. Rain soaking deep into the ground . . . We have no covering for our peaks. Send the snow to mantle their tops." *Snow! That's outrageous. It's June already.* But the words kept coming.

I e-mailed the prayer to family and friends and urged them to e-mail it to others. I don't know how many people prayed that day, but on June 4, I got an e-mail from my sister: "Missoula got six inches of snow." The next message was from a friend in Libby in the northwest corner of Montana: "It's pouring! We've been getting downpours all day!" I rushed outside and looked at the sky. Clouds—heavy gray ones, with rain. One, two, three drops falling ever so gently on my face, each one an answer to prayer.

Rush-Hour Prayer

by Connie Bergquist

———— ·❀· ————

Susanna, hurry up," I said to my seven-year-old daughter on yet another frantic weekday morning. "We're going to be late." I was a newly single mom with a full-time job and a split-second schedule I tried to stick to no matter what. Susanna wasn't a morning person, so keeping her on task at 6:30 AM was exasperating. She played with her toys, counted her Popsicle sticks, anything but get dressed. I'd lecture her all the way to school about being on time, which left us both miserable. I tried everything to make mornings go well—lunches packed, clothes laid out the night before—but Susanna didn't move any faster.

One morning I woke up fifteen minutes before my alarm. I was already worried about how the day would unfold. Why not pray? So I did, right then. *Lord, please give me patience. Help me let go of the need for everything to be perfect*. If Susanna's bed wasn't made or her hair had a few snarls, did it matter? Wasn't it more important to share a hug before school? Make time for the stuff that really mattered? That morning Susanna still dawdled, but I felt more at peace. I dropped her off at school, no tirade this time. I set my alarm fifteen minutes earlier the next day, and the next. Susanna didn't become a morning person, school still started at eight fifteen and I still had to be at work at eight thirty, but instead of lecturing her, I was able to calmly get her out the door. Soon our rides became filled with happy chatter.

Today Susanna's a college sophomore who wisely avoids enrolling in morning classes. And I'm a mom who's learned that life doesn't always go the way I plan. I'm much happier giving it over to God right when I wake up and letting Him take care of the rest of the day.

Fear Takes Flight

by Vincent Yeo

I'm a motivational speaker, flying all over the country giving speeches. But for years I had a terrible fear of flying. My hands would sweat and my pulse race the minute I reached the Jetway. *This is irrational*, I'd tell myself, but it made no difference. The fear was overwhelming. I'd grip the armrests till my knuckles turned white. Takeoffs and landings were particularly hard. The irony of giving speeches to help other people yet having such a crippling fear myself wasn't lost on me.

I began to pray every Sunday, asking God to remove the fear. But months passed and my fear remained. Then one Sunday, kneeling beside my wife in church, I looked up. At that moment, a man stood several rows in front of me. He turned and smiled at me, then walked up the aisle, stopped at my pew and handed me what appeared to be a business card, then he continued up the aisle. *How odd*, I thought. I finished my prayer, stood and glanced at the card. "Dear God," it read, "please protect me while I travel to do the work You've given me and bring me back home safely to my family." I turned to look for the man, but he was gone. "Maybe he was an angel," my wife said. I wasn't sure. But I tucked the card into my wallet.

On my next flight I pulled out the card and read it while waiting for takeoff. Though my pulse raced, I could feel my nerves calm. On the following flight, I felt less anxious. Finally, one day, without being aware of it, my fear left. No more gripping the armrests or sweaty palms.

The card is dog-eared and worn now, but it's still in my wallet. I don't know what ever happened to the man who gave it to me. But I know that that Sunday he was an answer to my prayer.

I Am Living, Breathing Proof

by Sandra Simpson LeSourd

---

*I*n the living room of a cozy ranch house nestled next to the rim-rock cliffs that border Billings, Montana, a group of women sat with clasped hands and bowed heads. "Dear Lord," Marlene said, "we're here to pray for Sandy. She's in deep trouble. She doesn't know we are praying for her, but Lord, we ask humbly that You be with her and strengthen her."

At that same moment, I sat in Warm Springs, Montana, staring through the grime-streaked windows of the State Hospital for Mental Disorders. My weight was over two hundred pounds, my skin was gray and my hair greasy—a sad situation for someone who, twenty-two years before, had represented her home state of Vermont at the Miss America Pageant in Atlantic City.

How had I gotten myself into such a miserable condition? There's a lot of scientific jargon to describe compulsive personalities like mine. My motto since my teen years had been: Anything worth doing is worth overdoing. I would tell people, "When my motor is running, I can't seem to shut it off."

And eventually my compulsive overdoing resulted in debilitating addictions to everything from alcohol, prescription drugs and nicotine, to overeating and out-of-control shopping sprees.

"It's time to start," said Marlene. They were meeting again as they did every Thursday morning, these ten or twelve women from the First United Methodist Church in Billings. After opening with songs of praise, there were prayers of thanksgiving—and then progress reports about the people they'd been praying for. The meetings generally lasted about two hours, each woman bringing a notebook to record the prayers they'd be making throughout the week. Special prayer attention was focused on the group's "Ten-Most-Wanted List," a list they had compiled, containing desperate cases of people most in need of the Lord: a teenager on drugs, a mother with Alzheimer's, a husband in the last stages of cancer, and a recent "most wanted" addition—Sandy.

So many people had tried unsuccessfully to help me: my family, friends, counselors and psychiatrists, including those at a treatment center where I'd spent a month. I put my head in my hands. It seemed hopeless. Could I ever go home? Would I ever be whole again?

Since the group believed in the power released by affirming the best in the person being prayed for, over and over they inserted my name into Scripture verses: "Strength and dignity are [Sandy's] clothing.... [Sandy] opens her mouth with wisdom, and the teaching of kindness is on her tongue.... Her children rise up and call her blessed" (Proverbs 31:25, 26, 28).

And then the women asked God "to transform Sandy, send Your emissaries across her path to witness to her, to free her from bondage."

I was in bondage—to a suicidal depression and spiritual darkness. Every time I closed my eyes, an inky black curtain fell across my conscious mind, and I was unable to summon any positive or pleasing visual images. It was terrifying to be lying in bed with my eyes closed and see nothing but forbidding night—or worse, evil, mocking faces.

One day a young woman named Karen entered the hospital and was assigned to a room adjacent to mine. Her fiancé, it was reported, had been killed in an accident. Karen was inconsolable. Over and over she kept crying out, "Help me, Jesus! Help me, Jesus!"

Karen's constant yelling was aggravating. And the worst thing was, she attached herself to me. I tried to avoid Karen, but she followed me, her dark brown eyes pleading for me to help her.

Then, on a sultry July night, I was tossing restlessly in my hospital bed, when I sensed a presence. I sat up. Karen was standing in the doorway, her white robe startlingly bright in the moonlight.

She approached my bed, crying softly. "Oh, Sandy, does Jesus love me? Does Jesus really love me?" I could tell from her pleading voice that this was the only thing in the world that mattered to her.

What to do? What to say? I longed to comfort this weeping young woman but felt incapable of reassuring anybody of anything. Yet I had to do something. Taking Karen in my arms, I stroked her damp hair. It had been a long time since I'd held anyone or offered comfort—I'd always been the one demanding it.

I cleared my throat awkwardly. "Yes, Karen," I said. "Jesus—"

I stopped in astonishment. My heart was beating furiously, I felt warm and cold at the same time. What was I saying to this young woman? Why were these

words having such power over her—and over me?
"Karen," I said. "Jesus loves you. He really does."

Her sobbing stopped in an instant. She wiped her eyes with the back of her hand, thanked me in a voice of childlike gratitude, and slipped out of my room and back to hers.

I lay back down, puzzled at the strange lightness, almost giddiness, that I was feeling. The room seemed filled with a fragrant coolness.

"[Sandy] opens her mouth with wisdom, and the teaching of kindness is on her tongue . . . . Her children rise up and call her blessed . . . ."

Thursday morning. The intercessors were meeting. "Dear Lord," Naomi said, leading the others in prayer, "God has not given [Sandy] a spirit of timidity, but of power and love and discipline" (2 Timothy 1:7 NAS). "And with his stripes [Sandy is] healed" (Isaiah 53:5 KJV).

A few days after Karen's nighttime visit to my room, she left the hospital just as suddenly as she had arrived. I puzzled about what had happened between us; for the first time in my long illness—and almost against my will—I seemed to have helped another person.

Was there something different happening to me? A glimmer of joy here, a flicker of wonder there? I'd been noticing the birds outside my window, a rose in a vase in the patients' lounge, the picture of a child in the recreation area.

I stared out the window into a small grassy courtyard. The morning sun had appeared over the building annex, casting shadows from a slatted roof overhang into my room. Across my skirt and onto the floor fell a pattern of stripes. Out of nowhere, words came into my mind: *And with His stripes we are healed.*

They sounded scriptural, but what did I know about the Bible? Could I have heard these words as a child in Sunday school? Strange, yet the words were strongly, deeply reassuring. Was it possible that I could get better after all?

Marge, Loretta, Eva, Dottie, Betty, Bess—the prayer witnesses were faithful to their tasks. Many of them prayed not only on Thursdays but on every day of the week too, sometimes out loud during morning and evening devotions, sometimes silently while waiting in line at checkout counters or sitting in traffic. Again and again their prayers went out: "[Sandy] can do all things through him who strengthens [her]" (Philippians 4:13 NAS).

To everyone's surprise, including my own, I was making such good progress that for the first time, the hospital staff felt I might make it on my own. A visit home was in order.

The first morning back in Billings in my own bed, I awoke terrified. How could I make up to my family for all my irresponsible behavior over the past fifteen years? Feelings of guilt and fear overwhelmed me. *Sleep in*, came the tempting voice inside my head. *Stay right here in bed*. That was the way I had handled things in the past.

But a new voice inside me spoke. *Get up and get going. Now!*

The old ways were entrenched, though, resistant to something new. I was afraid. No, I'd stay in bed today and start my new life tomorrow.

Get up. Do it now! The voice wouldn't stop—and I actually started to think I might enjoy getting on with my life. I got up, showered, put in a load of wash, made an appointment to have my hair cut and mopped the kitchen floor.

Major victories! As I moved from task to task, I was aided by a new inner feeling, a positive inner reinforcement that could be gentle and encouraging but at the same time insistent and strong. In the past my inner voice had always been negative, undermining and relentlessly critical. Now I felt a resolve and new sense of purpose that shocked me.

Another Thursday. For over a year the group in Billings had been praying for the woman with the severe problems of addiction. Once again they bowed their heads and said, "We know that God causes all things to work together for good to [Sandy] who [loves] Him" (Romans 8:28 NAS).

But at this meeting there was a difference: I was sitting among them.

On a bright June morning in 1979, I walked into a living room filled with smiling women who welcomed me warmly. My neighbor Kathy had invited me, and I perched nervously on the edge of a green sofa, waiting to see what all this "intercessory prayer" was about. I learned for the first time about the prayers that had gone up for me during my darkest days. I still needed much healing, but I was on my way.

Week after week I joined them in their prayers for others and for myself. Then, when I left Billings once again for a treatment center and halfway house, they continued their prayers. And later when I moved to Vermont to start a new life, I continued to call or write them. Their prayers were making a difference in my life, and I knew it.

Today I am living, breathing proof that prayers for others—intercessory prayers—are one of the most powerful tools that God has placed in our hands. My recovery did not take place in a month, or even a year. It was a long process. Even nowadays, every so often, the tendency toward addictive behavior beckons me back to the old habits. It's then that I say my own prayer: "I, Sandy, can do all things through Christ Who strengthens me." Then I bow my head, insert somebody else's name—and pass the prayer along for another.

The Everlasting Arms

by Frieda E. Nowland

When the doctor told me that my precious six-week-old son Paul was blind, I went into shock. I tried to pray, but for some reason I couldn't.

Hours passed and I still could not form words into prayer. Meanwhile. news of our baby's disability spread among our family, friends and church congregation. An army of prayer warriors carried their concern for Paul, my husband, and me to the Lord.

Two days later, while I was bathing Paul, something almost mystical happened, Ever so quietly and gently I was reminded of the Bible verse "...and underneath are the everlasting arms..." (Deuteronomy 33:27 NIV). I had the distinct feeling of being buoyed up, supported. And my depression began to lift.

Paul is an adult now. Though legally blind, he went to college and is employed; he can read with special magnifying glasses.

I discovered on that day long ago that even when you yourself cannot pray, the prayers of others can intercede for you. That barrage of prayers didn't change Paul's problem, but it changed me. Ever since, in good times and in bad, I've been sustained by the knowledge of His everlasting arms.

4
*I*NCREDIBLE *I*NTERVENTION

*T*he Lord your God is in your midst, a mighty one who will save; he will rejoice over you with gladness; he will quiet you by his love . . . ."

ZEPHANIAH 3:17 ESV

O Lord, sometimes we face impossible situations.
Help us remember that we're never alone and that You are
a gracious and compassionate God Who is able to intervene and deliver
us from all evil. Thank You for hearing us when we call to You!

Artful Reassurance

by Carolinda Jankel

My husband Bob had health problems, and it had gotten so bad he worried he might have to give up the job he loved, teaching art at a middle school. His longtime doctor had urged him to see a specialist, but Bob was really worried about finding the right person. "I don't know this new doc," he complained. "How do I know if he's right for me?"

I thought back to the beginning of our marriage, when we traveled to galleries and art fairs throughout California, selling Bob's work. We'd pack the car before dawn with his abstract paintings, along with a metal cash box for the money we hoped to make. Those were such carefree days. It was exciting to show his work and meet other artists, even if we didn't make many sales. What mattered was finding people who liked his work.

One time, at a street fair in Westwood, near UCLA, we'd sold nothing all day. We were packing up our car to leave when a young boy and his father came up to us. "How much is that one?" the man asked, pointing to the last painting we left out. We told him, and he asked if we had time to show them more. Did we ever! Our two patrons walked away with eight paintings! What a great feeling. "That," said Bob, during the drive home, "was a real Godsend."

So my heart ached for my husband when he finally went off to see the specialist. Bob looked so miserable that I said a prayer for him.

But he was different when he returned. Smiling, bright-eyed, a bounce in his step. "What happened to you?" I asked.

Bob told me that he had been reluctant to enter that specialist's office. He sat in the waiting room and flipped through some magazines for something to distract him. He glanced around the room at the other patients, at the receptionist, but he couldn't stop mulling over the difficult decisions he had to make about this specialist, his health, his job.

Then he looked up. And immediately he felt reassured. He knew he was in just the right place. There, hanging on the office walls, beautifully displayed, were eight paintings. Those same eight paintings we'd sold on that day so many years ago.

Leaf It to God

by Carol Gimbel

―――――

I dragged my rake through the leaves, thinking about how last fall Steve would have been here with me, helping out with Aunt Maudie's yard.

It had been five months since my husband's death from a heart attack. I struggled to go on. I'd prayed and prayed for relief from the gray sadness I seemed to live in. But it seemed impossible without Steve.

Tired, I knelt down to pluck leaves from my rake. That's when I noticed—my left hand, the hand where I wore the diamond ring Steve had given me, was bare. The ring must have fallen off while I was working.

I dropped to the ground and sifted through the pile of leaves, trying to stay calm and not start sobbing. I wasn't sure I could take another loss right then. Aunt Maudie asked her neighbors to help my search. One neighbor even walked the yard with a metal detector. We scoured the ground and leaf piles for hours. I knew for a fact that I'd been wearing it when I started raking. But the ring was gone.

Just like Steve, I thought, trudging into the house for dinner with Aunt Maudie, feeling more hopeless than ever. I took my place at the table, but I didn't feel like eating.

Aunt Maudie was having none of it. "Dear Lord," she said, praying boldly, "You know where that ring is and how much it means to Carol. I know You can bring it back to her if it is Your will. Amen."

We had gone over every square inch of that yard. Aunt Maudie had to know that her prayer was impossible. Yet here she was, after all the hopeless searching, still trusting that God could find it for me. If I had faith like that, I thought, I could even imagine going on without Steve.

After dinner I stepped out onto the back porch and looked out at the newly raked yard. Suddenly something flashed on the ground. *What's that? A bright twinkle, almost like . . .*

I stepped into the yard and bent down. My ring!

Impossible? No, prayer is never impossible. It just took losing Steve's ring for me to understand that even without Steve I am never alone.

GAL POWER

by Dorene Leake

⎯⎯ ⁓⁓⁓ ⎯⎯

I had moved clear across the state of Washington for a fresh start following a painful divorce, and I was struggling to settle in, feeling lost and alone. More than anything, I wanted to make some friends. So I'd finally worked up the nerve to visit this church one Sunday in my new town.

Lord, let me fit in here, I prayed, hesitating in the doorway. *Surround me with friends*. I took a deep breath and walked in. I spied two women about my age sitting together. "May I sit with you?" I asked.

"Of course," the woman with silvery curls responded. "I'm Naomi, and this is Bonny." I slipped in beside them.

When the service was over, I invited the two women to lunch, and over pizza I told them a little about myself.

Naomi's husband had recently passed away. "It's not easy being alone," she agreed.

"After my husband died, like you, I just up and moved," Bonny said.

"Maybe we should start a Bible study for women like us," I suggested.

"I would really love something social," Bonny said.

We racked our brains over the following days. "What if we invite women to join us once a month for prayer, games and refreshments?" I finally suggested.

"I'll host the first one," Naomi said. "But what should we call ourselves?"

We tossed around some ideas. Finally I said, "How about GALS—God's Amazing Love Sustains?" We laughed. Our very own acronym! Perfect. We listed the meeting in the church bulletin the next Sunday.

The following Wednesday, our first meeting, I worried that no one would show up. But one by one, the women arrived, some widowed, some divorced like me, filling Naomi's living room. We had a ball together!

Since that first meeting, we GALS have become like a second family: eating out together, going to the movies, calling each other, sharing our lives. We take care of each other in tough times too.

God has surrounded me with friends. More than that, He has shown me, through these wonderful women, how to live up to our group's name.

Strange Prompting in the Night

by Lynn B. Link

————— ◊ —————

With our four little children and two visiting nieces to tuck in, bedtime that night took a long time. Over each drowsy child I said a prayer, asking God to watch over them. Later, when my husband and I went to bed, I lay on the edge of sleep, lulled by the innocent noises drifting down the hallway: deep-sleep sighs, the mumbled words of dreamy conversations.

At four thirty I woke up abruptly. I heard a niece whimper. Suddenly I found myself out of bed, running down the hallway. But not to the room where my niece lay. Without knowing why, I ran to my children's bedroom on the other side of the house.

I stood in their doorway, hearing my heart pounding in my ears. Something bad was about to happen.

Seconds ticked by. The children went on sleeping peacefully in their bunk beds. All was so quiet. *Why did I run here? Am I dreaming?*

And then before my eyes the upper half of the bunk bed came apart. I rushed forward to catch the heavy mattress board and mattress before they crashed down onto my littlest one, Rachel, in the bottom bunk. I cried for help and my husband came; in a few moments all was set to right.

Andy and I stepped back. "Why were you in here?" he asked.

"I don't know."

"Thank God you were," Andy said. And then, with a smile, he added, "Listen, we're whispering. The kids never even woke up."

The Valentine Visitor

by Sandi Simpson

───※───

Valentine's Day Eve dawned bright and sunny last year, with orders pouring in to my new shop, Perfect Petals Florist. Working in the floral business for the last twenty-five years, I knew how to be prepared, especially for a day like Valentine's Day. *Everything's going just as I planned*, I thought. New customers were calling constantly and the computers were spitting out orders left and right. My delivery guys were set to handle the dozens of roses, teddy bears, balloons and arrangements with baby's breath and wildflowers.

But as the day wore on and the phone continued to ring off the wall, I knew I wouldn't have enough deliverymen to handle all the orders. I walked into the back room of my shop, passing by the flowers waiting to be sent out, and sank down at my desk. What if I couldn't deliver everything on time? Valentine bouquets that arrived on February 15 would be pretty useless, could even cause a lot of lovers' quarrels. *Lord*, I prayed, *I know how to run a shop. But this time it seems I underestimated the orders. I'm desperate! What do I do?* I sat there quietly, taking in the scent of the flowers.

The phone rang. Great, probably another order. But, no. It was a pleasant-sounding man who said, "I'm looking for a temporary delivery job. Do you need help?"

"Yes! Come in tomorrow." I hung up. Could this stranger possibly be right for the job?

The man showed up the next morning, nicely dressed, driving an SUV. He explained that he was a military chaplain recently discharged from the service. "Do you know the area?" I asked.

"Yep, grew up here," he said. "And my truck has a GPS tracking system."

"Perfect," I said, incredibly relieved.

I didn't miss a delivery that day. And I got a Valentine's gift of my very own—a deliveryman who called right when I needed his help most.

After the Fall

by Mary Lou Carney

My son Brett has always been our wild child. When he was little, he'd take the most outrageous dares. As a teen he got a four-wheeler and snuck it out at night to jump ditches along our country road. In short, Brett was the kind of son who kept this mother praying. I hoped Brett would outgrow his risky behavior. Then I could spend less time worrying (and praying for him). But Brett went into construction, starting his own company. He handled heavy equipment and climbed on all kinds of structures. Still, when he got married last year, I told myself, *Things will settle down now.*

Then Brett took on his first big commercial job, a strip mall. Each morning on my way to work I passed Brett's site. I watched as the lot became piles of dirt, then rows of foundation walls. One day I saw a huge crane towering above the structure. It could only mean one thing: Brett would be high above the ground, setting roof trusses. *Keep him safe, Lord*, I prayed. *Let Your angels attend him*. I kept repeating those words.

Hours later, sitting at my desk, I was still thinking about Brett. Then my phone rang. My worst fear had come true. Brett had fallen thirty-five feet. He was in the ER. My husband Gary and I rushed to the hospital. Brett was lying on a gurney, in pain, but still joking. After tests, the doctor told us, "He's very bruised and will feel very sore. But amazingly he has no broken bones. He'll be fine." That day Gary and I visited the site and stood where Brett had fallen. The broken truss lay in pieces. And just to the left of it was a cement wall. If Brett had shifted in his fall . . . I couldn't bear the thought.

I suspect I'll never spend less time praying for Brett. But his safe landing tells me I can worry a little less.

NIGHT LINE

by Lillian Robertson

———∿∿∿———

I awoke with a start. Outside it was still dark. I'd just had the most disturbing dream about a young man. I knew he was in grave danger. It was the height of the Vietnam War and my son John was serving in the Air Force. But, somehow, I knew the danger wasn't about him. It was about his childhood friend James Rudy Bailey Jr. I was sure of it.

But why James? I hadn't seen him since he was about eight years old. His family had moved across town years ago. I didn't even know where James was anymore.

God, I prayed, tears rolling down my cheeks, *I don't know what's wrong, but please, please help James. He's in terrible danger.* I prayed and prayed, never moving from my spot in bed. My husband Flavil didn't stir. Hours passed, but I never tired. I couldn't even picture

James's face, but I knew he was in dire straits. I kept praying.

Dawn finally came, the light creeping through the windows, when I felt released from the fear I'd had all through the night. I knew that James was safe just as surely as I'd known he was in danger. *Thank You, Lord*, I prayed, *for sending me to James's aid through prayer.* Later that day I told Flavil about my dream.

Two weeks later, Flavil was in a restaurant, getting coffee. There sat James's dad James Sr. Flavil sat down to talk with him. "How's James doing?" he asked.

"He's okay now," James Sr. replied.

"What do you mean?" Flavil asked.

"Well, he's serving with the army in Vietnam. One night two weeks ago, he got trapped alone behind enemy lines and almost got captured. He barely made it back to his unit. Threw a real scare into him. Us too."

Flavil looked at him, wide-eyed. Then he ordered another cup of coffee and told James Sr. all about my night of prayer.

A New Trust

by Mimi Jones Hedwig

———— ·ɱ· ————

Rufus, my golden retriever, and I sat in the yard that summer evening a year ago, enjoying the sunset. The yard wasn't fenced; dense woods ran right up to the lawn. I'd snapped a long leash onto Rufus' collar. If he strayed, I could easily grab it before he got into any trouble. Suddenly Rufus' head jerked up. Before I could react, he took off. I ran after him, but he disappeared into the woods. I called, to no avail. Night was falling. I thought of Rufus dragging his lead. What if it gets snagged and he's trapped? I shuddered to think what coyotes might do to a helpless dog. I dashed into the house to call my friend Susan.

Susan and I work together on a prayer request line and she's also a dog lover. She pulled into the drive minutes later. For the next six hours we crisscrossed the woods, calling Rufus' name. "What if I never find him?" I said, fighting tears.

"Don't worry," Susan said. "Just pray, like we tell people on the prayer line." Pray. Why didn't that occur to me? I thought about the times I'd spoken with callers and told them God hears and answers prayers. There in the moonlit woods I knelt down. *Lord, please keep Rufus safe. Help me find him.*

At 2:00 AM, I sent Susan home. Tired and discouraged, I lay on my bed and prayed again. Then, faintly, I heard faraway barking. I got up, grabbed a flashlight and bolted out the door. Calling Rufus' name, I ran into the woods. Suddenly I saw two glowing eyes staring at me through the trees. "Rufus?" I whispered. There he was, sitting patiently, his leash wrapped tightly around a tree. I knelt down and hugged him. How long had he been there? I'd wonder later. All I could think about now was the tremendous gift I'd been given: proof that God hears and answers prayer.

Right On Time

by Blake Thompson

--- ꝏ ---

I'm a die-hard 'Bama fan, especially when it comes to the Iron Bowl, the end-of-season matchup of Auburn and Alabama. Even when I was in the National Guard serving as a combat medic, I followed every game. Now that my wife Brook and I have three kids, we don't get to as many games. But if tickets come our way, we grab them. Last year, though, we'd waited too long to get tickets to the Bowl and they were a few hundred dollars. "Maybe we should pray for tickets," Brook said.

I looked at her, thinking she was joking. She wasn't. "I hate to bother God with something as trivial as that."

"At least we could leave it in God's hands," Brook pressed. I agreed. "Lord, if You could get us tickets to Saturday's game, we'd be grateful," I said.

That Thursday a friend called. She had an extra pair of tickets! But they were deep in Auburn territory.

"We'll manage," I said.

So there we were with our crimson shirts amid all that Auburn orange. During the first quarter, I heard a commotion two rows down. A woman screamed that her husband was having a heart attack. I rushed down and saw an older man slumped over, his face blue. I've seen that same deadly pallor before. I leapt over the seats and started CPR. *Come on.* I kept doing compressions. Soon, paramedics arrived with a defibrillator and whisked him away.

The man, Herman Culpepper, survived his heart attack. The doctor told him about the Alabama fan who saved his life. Talk about being in the right place at the right time. But I should've realized that no prayer is a "bother" because we never know how God will choose to answer—only that He does.

Safely Home

by Mary Pettit Holmes

―――――― ⁓ ――――――

I had to stay late that evening at the bloodmobile, where I am a registered nurse working with the American Red Cross. By the time I trudged out to my car, it was dark, and fog was rolling in. I had an hour's drive home to our small town nestled near the base of the coastal range.

The traffic was light, which was good, because the fog was getting heavier. I could barely see the white line at the edge of the freeway and the streetlamps that lit it. Then I turned off onto our country road. Ten more miles to drive on a narrow, twisting road with deep ditches and a stream alongside.

"Help me, Lord," I prayed. Recently in church we had been discussing the use of mental imaging while praying, Now I visualized Jesus sitting next to me in the passenger seat. I poured out my fears to Him.

Hugging the steering wheel, I stared at the eerie whiteness. Suddenly ahead of me I saw the red taillights of another car. Slowly I drew closer. The red taillights were on an orange pickup being hauled by a tow truck. I was relieved. Undoubtedly the pickup was being taken to the garage in Forest Grove. If I followed it, I could make it home.

We came to Main Street—but we passed the repair shop. The tow truck drove on. It kept going. To my amazement, it turned into the dead-end road where we lived. With a sigh of relief, I turned into our driveway, then quickly got out to thank the driver of the tow truck that had led me home.

There was no driver. There was no tow truck. It had not turned around to exit from the dead end. I stood staring into the silent fog at the end of our road.

Wednesday Night Special

by Jackie Scott

$\mathcal{E}$very week a bunch of us have dinner. Not at the food court or the local steak house, but at church. For a few nights, at least, everyone eats healthy. That can be a struggle, as my daughter Diane and I know a little better than most. But we found a solution.

Flash back five years. I weighed 250 pounds. Diane was over 350. She couldn't even use a normal scale. When I met my husband Brett in college, I had been a svelte 127. But I would think nothing of eating fast food every day. I never exercised, and eventually my metabolism couldn't keep up with my appetite. Diane copied my eating and exercise habits. She'd just graduated college heavier than I had ever been. How was she going to have a normal life?

That summer the three of us moved from Michigan to Kentucky for Brett's new job. Lexington was wonderful. We joined the church choir, made new friends. But my weight caused some embarrassing situations. Like when I visited the DMV to get a Kentucky license.

"Age?" The woman asked. "Forty-seven," I replied. "Height?" "Five-two." "Weight?" I stared at the ground. "One-seventy-five," I mumbled. The woman gave me a look but didn't say anything. I knew what she was thinking: yeah, right.

I told Brett what had happened. "Maybe now is the perfect time for all of us to go on a diet," Brett said. We'd tried all the diets before: the Zone, Sugar Busters. We didn't need a diet; we needed a miracle.

In church that week I prayed, *God, please help me and Diane lose weight. Please let it be different this time.* As soon as I finished, a thought jumped into my head. What will you do differently this time? Why had all our diets failed? Why had we?

I hit the books. I found out it all seemed to come down to two things: calories and exercise. We burn about 1,800 calories a day; if you eat fewer calories than you burn, you lose weight. Simple. Most diets cut too many calories. We're starving! That's not healthy. The key was making smart food choices.

Diane and I started cooking our own calorie-conscious meals. We studied nutrition labels on every package. We walked. Whenever one of us was tempted to wolf down a bag of chips, we had the other to keep us in line. We were losing weight slowly and steadily. Eventually I'd lost almost a hundred pounds. Diane had lost nearly two hundred!

"You guys look great!" our choir buddy David told Brett one morning after church. Then he turned serious. "I wish I could lose weight. The doctor says I'm at risk for another stroke. I've been praying for a miracle." The same miracle I prayed for.

I called him up. "We're making dinner tonight," I said. "Why don't you and your wife Jackie join us?"

We started cooking and eating meals with David and Jackie. They lost weight. Soon other people in the choir were asking, "Hey, can we join you guys too?"

That's how our dinners got started. We'd cook healthy meals and serve them at church five days a week. Chicken simmered in a honey-mustard glaze. Creamy orzo pilaf and roasted asparagus. Soon everyone got involved. Later we took over the regular dinners before Wednesday night services for the whole congregation. Not only were we eating better but we were encouraging one another in good habits. Just what a church should do. The minister himself came up to thank me. "My wife lost sixty-five pounds! She's so happy, confident, full of energy. We're all eating healthier."

God gave us good food to eat, we just have to make the right choices.

LITTLE BOY LOST

by Paul Humphrey

—⁓—

I hurried up the lane toward the crowd gathered at the little farmhouse near the town of Salem in southern Indiana. The road was lined with cars and trucks with license plates from Indiana, Ohio and Kentucky. The time was seven thirty and the December night was black and frigid. Ahead, revolving lights flashed from police cars. Television crews hunched against a windchill of fourteen degrees as they unwound cables and set up equipment. Reporters stamped their feet against the cold as they waited for word—any word— about little four-year-old Dale Coats, who had wandered off from home and was lost.

I strode past the troopers puffing clouds of steam as they compared notes with search parties. I thought of how I would feel if my little five-year-old Amanda had disappeared in the dark forest surrounding this area. That's why, when I left my home about ten miles from here, I explained to her, "If you were lost in the woods I'd want everybody in the world looking for you."

But that wasn't the only reason I'd come. Even though there were seven hundred people out searching, I actually thought I could be the hero of the hour and be the one to find the boy. After all, Grandpa's old farm was nearby, and for years I'd tramped the surrounding hills and hollers looking for mushrooms or tracking deer. I was an experienced woodsman and proud of it. Maybe too proud.

I walked past the police cars and knocked on the farmhouse door. Dale's mother, thin, in her twenties, eyes swollen, told me in a shaking voice, "He's been missing since noon. My husband and I were stripping tobacco in the barn, and Brother—that's what Dale answers to—" Her voice choked. "Brother said he was hungry. I told him to 'Go on up to the house, I'll be there in a bit.' But"—she swallowed hard—"when I came in, he wasn't there. His daddy hollered and hollered for him. But nothing. Then we saw the dogs were gone too. We've been searching ever since."

The little fella had been missing almost eight hours! How long could a four-year-old survive this freezing weather?

An icy rain began to fall. I was wearing my Naval Reserve foul-weather gear and ice-fishing boots. But Brother, according to his mom, wore only light clothing and tennis shoes.

Before heading into the woods, I looked around the barn. It just might be that the boy was nearby all the time. I remembered how I used to climb into our combine and hide in the hopper. Hope flickered through me and I prayed, "Lord, let me find him right here." My heart beat faster as I swept the hopper with my flashlight, but it was empty.

"Help me find him, Lord," I prayed as I struck out into the forest. I pushed through the brush, feeling more and more confident that if anyone was to find Brother it was going to take someone with real woods savvy and a tracking nose, someone like me. All around me shouts of "Brother! Brother!" rang out. Flashlights bobbed like fireflies. I knelt down looking for tracks. The top inch of soil hadn't frozen as yet. In it I could see tracks of a buck, a raccoon, several dogs and one coyote. But no tracks of a little boy wearing tennis shoes.

For two hours I combed the woods, then in a field, I bumped into Dale's dad. He spoke to several of us grouped around him. "Boys, I believe he's up there somewhere." He pointed to the dark hills, silhouetted in the distance. "He comes out with me to cut wood, and when he wants to go home, I tell him to go on top of the hill and look for the barn. Brother knows our house is on a hill."

I teamed up with Jim Watson, a deputy friend, and I searched the higher ground while Jim covered the lower ground. By two in the morning we had found no sign of the boy.

The rain turned to wet snow and we headed back to the Coatses' farmyard to see if there was any news. Folks stood rubbing their hands over fires burning in fifty-gallon drums. Some county conservation officers handed out walkie-talkies to groups of searchers and pointed to various circles drawn on a map.

Would Brother still be alive after fifteen hours in this freezing cold? From my Naval Reserve training I knew how deadly hypothermia could be, especially for a little tyke in light clothing. Jim and I took off again.

Around four thirty in the morning there was some news. A bloodhound brought in from Louisville had found the boy's scent. Following it, searchers had found Brother's cap and a broken shoestring. Then there had been tracks near the bottoms that led to a creek. Cave-ins along the bank indicated that the boy had fallen into the creek more than once but had climbed out.

After that the bloodhound lost Brother's scent. Lost too was the optimism that had seemed to be so prevalent earlier. Men slowly shook their heads.

At six thirty I stood by the creek with a group of conservation officers. A massive hill on the other side of the stream loomed against the graying sky. *He knows home is on a hill*, echoed in my mind. Something inside me told me I should climb it.

However, the conservation people, faced with two thousand acres of land, thought it best to concentrate on where his tracks were found. "No, he'd have been too tired to climb that hill," someone argued.

"He may be tired, but he's homesick," I said as I struck up the hill by myself. By now I was getting pretty tired. My sides ached and my throat was raw from shouting. But as I struggled up the incline, I kept crying, "Brother!" Finally I stopped and leaned against a tree, breathing heavily. Maybe the conservation officers were right. Maybe the boy would have been too tired to make it.

Suddenly I was startled by the sound of a high-pitched "Eek, eek." It came from the shadowed trees ahead and I began running to it. It was the boy! I knew it was. But when I came to the trees my hopes crashed. Above me, two branches scraped in the wind, squeaking, "Eek, eek."

I slumped against a mossy trunk, desolate. It was now morning, and all I could see was another hill. And another. A crow called faintly in the distance. The rank, decayed leaves and vegetation smelled of death.

So much for me and my "experienced" woodsmanship. I had failed. As the cold wind sighed through the trees, I felt crushed, helpless. I sank to my knees on the forest floor. All night I had tried to stay dry, but now the icy wetness of the ground soaked through my pants and I didn't care. I bowed my head and folded my numbed hands together. "Lord," I said out loud, "maybe I was thinking more about myself. Maybe I was thinking more about what a good woodsman I was and what a hero I'd be, rather than about that lost little boy. But, Lord, please, let somebody find him. Don't let him die out here."

Rising up, I began walking again. Now I wasn't feeling any panic. Without any sense of particular direction, I let my feet carry me from ridge to ridge.

As I pushed through bracken a faint sound caught my ear. A kind of squeak. I stopped.

Was it another tree? Me wheezing? Or could it be . . . ?

Again it sounded, and I ran screaming "Brother!" into the woods ahead. I stopped to listen. Nothing.

I called again. Still nothing. I ran back toward the open field where I first heard the noise. "Brother!" I called.

From somewhere came a sound like "Hea."

It had to be Brother. It had to be!

"I hear you, little buddy," I shouted. "I hear you. Just keep calling until I find you."

"Hea . . . hea . . ." came the faint words. They seemed to be coming from somewhere above me. A hill. Of course. I ran toward a barbed-wire fence, pushed down the rusty strand and climbed through. As the wire squeaked against the fence post I heard a dog barking.

"Brother!" I called.

"Hea." The sound was louder. I crashed through waist-high foxtail weeds but still couldn't see anything.

"Brother?"

"Hea," sounded close behind me.

I wheeled, and there before me was a sight I'll never forget. In a hollow, two dogs lay curled around the body of a little boy. The boy was motionless.

As I approached, my heart hammering, one of the dogs, a Border collie, slowly rose to its feet, black-and-white hair bristling, teeth bared. It growled, then, as if sensing I was there to help, it moved aside. That's when I saw Dale Coats's face.

No wonder he couldn't call out clearly. His lips were cracked open and bleeding from the cold. His head lay on a smaller brown-and-black dog who peered up at me with black marble eyes. Dale's blue eyes followed me too, but he didn't move. Then, I saw he couldn't; his hands were crossed against his chest, seemingly frozen into position.

"I've come to take you home, little buddy," I said. "Your mama's looking for you."

I knelt down and lifted his head from the dog. His hair and the dog's fur had frozen together. I pried apart bits of ice, fur and hair. When I separated them, the smaller dog, something like a dachshund, rose unsteadily to its feet and looked up at me. Its job was done; its warmth was no longer needed.

Quickly both dogs took off. I wrapped my coat around Dale, took his body into my arms and started running toward the road.

Well, that's the story of the little boy who got lost on a cold December day. I'm happy to say that Brother bounced back to health quickly, the way little boys often do, and life on the Coatses' farm took on its normal pace again. The two dogs, by the way, found their own way back that morning—they could have taken off for home for food and warmth anytime, but they didn't.

And as for me, my life went back to its normal pace too, except that I think I'm a little different. Let me put it this way: When some of my pals asked me, "Tell us how you found the little guy, Paul," I replied, "Fellows, let me tell you about the One Who really found him."

A NOTE
FROM THE EDITORS

We hope you enjoy *Mysterious Ways: Incredible Answers to Prayer*, created by Guideposts Books and Inspirational Media. In all of our books, magazines and outreach efforts, we aim to deliver inspiration and encouragement, help you grow in your faith, and celebrate God's love in every aspect of your daily life.

Thank you for making a difference with your purchase of this book, which helps fund our many outreach programs to the military, prisons, hospitals, nursing homes and schools. To learn more, visit GuidepostsFoundation.org.

We also maintain many useful and uplifting online resources. Visit Guideposts.org to read true stories of hope and inspiration, access OurPrayer network, sign up for free newsletters, join our Facebook community, and follow our stimulating blogs.

To order your favorite Guideposts publications, go to ShopGuideposts.org, call (800) 932-2145 or write to Guideposts, PO Box 5815, Harlan, Iowa 51593.